BIG

FUCKING

SECRET

.COM

The Big Fucking Secret

HOW TO LIVE A KICK-ASS LIFE
DESPITE ALL THE BULLSHIT

Eli Rook

Copyright © 2011, 2012 by Eli Rook, LLC All rights reserved. "Eli Rook", "The Big Fucking Secret", and "Control Existence" are a trademarks of Eli Rook, LLC

"The Big Fucking Secret: How To Live A Kick-Ass Life Despite All The Bullshit" (Final Rough Draft of Final Beta Version w/omission of Chapter 8).

Updated version info at BigFuckingSecret.com

Limit of Liability/Disclaimer of Warranty: While the publisher and author have used their best efforts in preparing this book, they make no representations or warranties with respect to the accuracy or completeness of the contents of this book and specifically disclaim any implied warranties of merchantability or fitness for a particular purpose. No warranty may be created or extended by sales representatives or written sales materials. The advice and strategies contained herein may not be suitable for your situation. Neither the publisher nor author shall be liable for any loss of profit or other commercial damages, including but not limited to special, incidental, consequential, physical, or other damages. The Big Fucking Secret is not a medical device. It is not intended to treat, cure, or prevent any illness or disease. You are not guaranteed to receive any specific results or monetary gains from the application of its contents. All results are based on your own personal efforts and results vary based on each individual's personal situations and circumstances.

ISBN: 0984743510

ISBN-13: 978-0984743513

CHAPTER LOCATIONS

Dedication	i
The Big Fucking Secret	1
INTRODUCTION	7
Chapter 1	17
Chapter 2	31
Chapter 3	43
Chapter 4	55
Chapter 5	69
Chapter 6	87
Chapter 7	109
Chapter 8	129
Chapter 9	133
Chapter 10	143
Chapter 11	155
Conclusion	165
Illuminations	169
Word of Advice	211

DEDICATION

*To everyone who made
this book a #1 Best Seller...*

You are all true champions.

*Thank you for your
love and support!*

"Goodbye Pathological Age"
by Eli Rook

It's time to say goodbye,
My dear Pathological Age,

We had our fun,
And the laughs were rich,

But it's time to say good bye.

You were the Age in which I came to be,
When I joined this bizarre civilization,

You tested my might each step of the way,
You forced me to solve the equation,

For so long I tried to fight you,
I tried with all my might,

But I've changed my mind,
For good this time...

I choose to say good bye.

The solution to the problem,
Was right in front of my eyes,

Hidden in plain sight,
Vast riches in disguise,

With a gentle touch of poise,
I shall lift your convincing veil,

To ascend into the field of love,
To meet mountains I shall scale,

To become ONE... finally,
With all that is surely real.

(To manifest all those dreams,
You always tried to steal.)

One last kiss my lovely,
Just one, for old time's sake,

Before I disperse your particles,
And finally stand awake,

I won't be working within you,
Because your subjects are leaving too,

They're fleeing your control grid,
And there's nothing you can do.

It's paradoxical how,
We never needed you.

It was YOU who needed us,
To constantly abuse,

But it was us who created you…
And your appetite to consume,

So thank you for all the survival pressures,
They gave us the power to choose.

Now that we choose to say good bye,
With your memory fresh in our minds,

Your shattered visage is already fading,
Disappearing back in time,

It's almost like you never existed,
And we've become more and more the wise,

We'll forget you and go on without you,
Living our exhilarating lives.

So I'm just checking in, this one last time,
To acknowledge you were once part of my life,

To show you that I have no animosity,
No tension to unwind,

You simply don't exist,
In the stars upon which I dine,

> *So let's just keep it short and sweet…*
> *It's time to say "Good bye"*

Eli Rook

THE BIG FUCKING SECRET

You are God.

But you're convinced that you're not, and that's what this book will help you overcome.

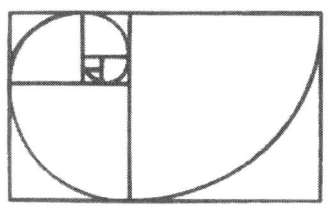

This book is designed to improve your cognition of the role you play throughout the existence field, and increase your ability to harness the power you've always had, but haphazardly use.

As you read and re-read The Big Fucking Secret, you'll endeavor through a series of exploratory *quantum crossings*, bringing you into a more frequent and consistent fifth dimensional orientation with reality.

From there, you'll work in harmony with other conscious beings to rapidly improve the conditions for life on planet Earth, and witness humanity thriving beyond the constipated *old world* you perceive today.

As you experience vibrant health, surging prosperity, and safety in *the new world order*, problems you observe will increasingly vanish – first slowly, then with more intensity – until you suddenly look back at the hazy memory of what you experienced in the past as being bizarre and unreal.

You'll then enthusiastically cast away the faintest acknowledgment of how life on planet Earth once was, and proceed to enjoy eternal physical and spiritual fulfillment in the *Civilization of Luminiferous Ascension*.

The Big Fucking Secret

Begin reading this book making no assumptions about the contents contained herein. Cast no doubt upon the bold claims issued in its opening paragraphs.

Forge onward challenging the author to deliver on these claims, and see for yourself whether or not you are effected in the manner proposed...

Upon reading the entire book cover-to-cover a second time, confidence in your power to control existence will reach an all-time high, and you'll feel like you truly know everything you need to know, in order to do everything you need to do.

With these feelings getting bigger and bigger, everything in your life will begin to shift in dramatically different ways, and the quantum crossings you experience will continue to become more frequent, and more apparent.

With the increased frequency of these quantum crossings into a new world, your old world "quantum triangulation" will naturally blur into oblivion, and the unfavorable residual effects of your lower dimensional orientation with reality will continue to vanish...

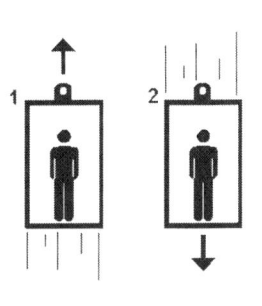

(The horrors of the past will all but disappear from your life experience =)

The shift in triangulation you experience will dramatically improve your career, your relationships, your personal happiness, and your ability to *consciously* control existence in your favor – enabling you to become more of the person you truly deserve to be.

2

Eli Rook
You Are God Within The Matrix Of Multidimensional Consciousness

As a multidimensional conscious being, you've been traversing an endless array of "alternate realities", ever since you became conscious.

As you read The Big Fucking Secret, you'll not only become more aware of this fact, but you'll gain even more awareness of the fact that you've been controlling your navigation 100% of the time.

Reflecting upon that, you'll increasingly understand that you lived most of your life under the illusion your efforts only effected the world around you *some of the time*.

This book has been custom-built to strip away those illusions, so you can finally see reality for what it really is *(your own personal playground =)*

The information presented in these pages was uniquely formatted to induce quantum crossings from your current fourth dimensional orientation with reality *(in which you've been stuck most of your life)*, into a destined fifth dimensional orientation with reality – where you consciously control existence to your favor (eternally).

This book is dynamically different than other books you've read about spirituality, The Law of Attraction, quantum physics, or self-development disciplines...

The Big Fucking Secret

That's because every page, every paragraph, and every last sentence was custom-crafted to facilitate your induction into the Civilization of Luminiferous Ascension.

Linguistic patterning, charged with energetic frequencies, are used to automatically guide you in the process of reprogramming your mind, and DNA, for this self-enacted higher dimensional immersion.

By simply reading the book twice, the series of exploratory quantum crossings you'll endure will activate "legacy pathways" in the brain, and establish a 5th dimensional "ascension switch" you can flip at any time.

Read "The Big Fucking Secret" cover-to-cover... then read it again.

It's a quick, illuminating read, and it's compatible with most honest religious principles, rational philosophical constructs, and evolved scientific knowledge available on planet Earth today. (To the reader who openly tests their own beliefs from time to time, it will be enormous fun.)

Certain methods of conceptual "hide-and-go-seek" exist throughout the work, which push the reader into new (and sometimes uncomfortable) realms of *knowledge integration*. It's also layered with *seeming contradictions* specifically postured to neutralize neurological "blockages" and unhealthy constructs you've acquired throughout your life.

Thus, *if you are teachable* – if you hold your defenses at bay, and allow the psychoactive energy of these words to produce their intended result, the quantum position you currently occupy will immediately shift into a position holding far more favorable advantages.

But do keep in mind, this book is only a utility...

It is ultimately YOU who controls every event transpiring in your life experience.

It is YOU who initiates that rush inside...

It is YOU who commands forth the harmonic pulsation of your *best life* to manifest.

And therein lies the "big fucking secret" chosen by the authors of this book to be its main subject.

You are God - in every sense of the word.

And you control the entire realm of existence in which your life expands...

Being convinced otherwise is the factor you now aim to remedy, and The Big Fucking Secret is designed to help you succeed.

The Big Fucking Secret

Eli Rook

Forge onward, reading *quickly*. Do not stop to intellectualize the contents presented. Relieve your conscious mind's tendency to evoke confusion, and trust that your brain is designed to naturally process the information correctly.

The first reading should be brisk and speedy, so any alpha blockages you may unknowingly possess will be bypassed.

Upon the second reading, feel free to deconstruct and dissect everything you learned, digging into each integrated concept from a 5th dimensional orientation.

- *When you come across a word you don't know, write it down, and look it up in a dictionary prior to your second reading.*
- *When you have an "a-ha moment", write it down in your own words to better serve your memory.*
- <u>*Use white paper and blue ink.*</u> *Do not type your cognitions into a computer!*

As you encounter energetic experiences, shifts in your conscious orientation, or phenomenon unfolding in your life experience, you may share them privately by emailing feedback@bigfuckingsecret.com, or publicly at http://bigfuckingsecret.com/social

The Big Fucking Secret

INTRODUCTION

It doesn't matter where on Earth you live, what race or bloodline you descended from, how much education you've received, or the number of years your current life experience has persisted. You are a conscious being, you have power, and it's your nature to seize that power. (Such is the nature of every conscious being here on Earth, and throughout the cosmos.)

Until now, you lived most of your life convinced you were just a poor, helpless mortal, having no control over the situations and circumstances you experienced since your birth.

You may have looked to the future, suspecting you'd have little or no control over the situations and circumstances you'd encounter until your death...

This is because, *at some point during your journey*, you forgot the fact that you were God... or you were somehow convinced by others that you were not God.

The fact that you remain convinced that you are not God, *(in ways which we'll discuss throughout the following chapters)* is the quintessential factor holding you back from getting everything you want. Knowing this, and holding an inherent ability to expand your awareness about the true nature of your being, you have the capacity to get what you want, given that it exists within the fifth dimension of endless potentiality.

The Big Fucking Secret
SO WHAT DO YOU WANT?

Do you want a lush, pulsating stream of synchronicity illuminating your life as each new day arrives?

Do you want to enjoy an endless sequence of serendipitous events unfolding all around you, everywhere you go?

How about knowing that you're living on the CUTTING EDGE, enjoying the fulfillment of your purpose in life, and knowing all your efforts are making the world a better place?

If so, it's no mistake you've acquired this book.... In fact, there are no mistakes in life whatsoever!

Everything that happens in your life is derived from your innate control over the entire existence field.

Do you want to consciously use your personal power to transform the entire world around you so each day is spent living life to the fullest, engulfed in the magic of your experience?

Do you want to reach a point where you are so deeply immersed in the blessings and abundance of each exhilarating moment life delivers that you make a complete *quantum leap* out of the old bizarre earth-bound civilization of crime, disease, and death -- into a new world of prosperity, sovereignty, and safety?

Good!

Eli Rook

This book is going to rock your world!!

Even having average intelligence, average physical abilities, and an average income, anyone who understands and acts on The Big Fucking Secret can readily do things others would consider to be outrageously *unaverage*...

It's your destiny to hit a non-stop winning streak in the game of life – thus you've manifested the inspiration to enable you to accomplish such a feat in the knowledge you'll gather throughout the pages of this book.

Quickly read The Big Fucking Secret from cover-to-cover, ignoring any ideas that don't agree with your own.

As you read, you'll clearly understand how you *already* use your power to control reality, and how you've been *unconsciously* using this power since you became conscious.

Then, you'll begin using your power CONSCIOUSLY to manifest specific desires you hold, by pleasurably and painfully changing in ways that enable you to sustain a consistent quantum triangulation upon the core path toward who-you-are-meant-to-be.

Upon reading the book a second time you'll experience a revelation that will change your life...

Everything will come together and you'll feel total clarity, total symmetry, and total control of existence (which is how you're supposed to feel all the time!)

Then you'll go on to live a kick-ass life in the new world order.

The Big Fucking Secret
What does your future look like?

You've read about other individuals - just like you - who traveled the world, made tons of money, and gave tons of money away.

They have great health, great energy, great sex, great stories, and great big smiles on their faces!

What kind of life would you be living if you could choose to do anything you wanted?

Would you just want to feel happy?

Would you live each day without a care in the world, doing something you really love?

Would you volunteer, work for a charity, or help out in some way? Would you take up art, or maybe travel the world?

Would you want to spend time with like-minded people, and do things that have never been done before?

What would you do?

In the past, you've created larger-than-life experiences, you've become lucky, you've been able to "get lucky", to overcome setbacks, to win against all odds, and create situations and circumstances in life during which you felt happy and fulfilled.

Just as often, you frequently used your power to create situations and circumstances that worked to your ultimate *disadvantage*.

The whole time you lived life convinced you were not God, you faced some pretty tough circumstances and situations (and it's no surprise!) When you refuse to accept the fact that you are God, or you allow others to convince you that you're not God, life never turns out the way you want it to. But when you just accept the fact that you ARE God and you can't be convinced otherwise, you end up learning how to create *real* magic in your life – on autopilot.

The more times you experience your own personal magic in life, the more you realize that you are God...

It's <u>YOU</u> who controls existence!

That realization is your foundational vantage point, where you can harness all the power you need to manifest all your desires – *regardless of how seemingly impossible they might be in the minds of others.*

You'll harness even more power as you practice, accelerating the ascent toward a complete 5th dimensional orientation with reality – a COMPLETE awareness that you are God...

From there, you'll develop new conceptualizations of everything happening at the smallest unit of existence – down below the smallest quantum particle – out to the endless expanding eternal multiverse (and everything you know in between)!

You'll find peace in understanding your cosmic role throughout the existence field, and how to consciously use your mind, brain, and body to customize life's vortex *in real-time* - for prosperity, safety, health, and happiness.

The Big Fucking Secret

You can easily feel good about yourself, your friends, your family, your community, society, and the world around you because you have the power to customize reality on Earth any way you please - *regardless of how its conditions currently appear!!*

What do you expect will happen when enough people collectively use their power to shift everything they experience on your planet *away* from what they don't want, *toward* what they do want?

Will the world "change"?

"Sure."

Will the world change for the better?

"Most undoubtedly."

Are YOU ready to change the world?

Here's the shocking secret...

"You're already doing it!"

(And you've BEEN DOING IT ever since you became conscious.)

Change in the "world" has nothing to do with other people... It has everything to do with how other people are effected by the change you conduct in your own life experience... And the only thing hindering this change is the fact that <u>*you're still convinced that you're not God*</u>*!"*

By fully understanding the previous statement, you'll acquire the illuminating cognition that your own personal transformation is subtly changing the world around you.

Eli Rook

Mastering that, you'll digitally program your mind to *quantum leap* into a new world of prosperity, happiness, and safety.

You'll begin to notice changes unfolding all around you, and situations and circumstances you encounter clearly working to your advantage more and more – as if by magic.

But it's not magic...

It's just you! (Because you are God)

Read The Big Fucking Secret cover-to-cover... Then read it once more.

As you reach the finish line you'll fully understand how your pulsation of energy controls the existence field, and you'll land in this new world, knowing all you need to know, in order to become more and more of the person you're meant to be...

(Alternatively, you could give up now, put the book down, and go back to living the fantasy life you've always lived - convinced you're just a random soul in a mortal meat suit, drifting from life to life, down on your luck because you have no real power over what the future truly holds.)

You won't be doing that of course...

You're genuinely eager to find out more about how to start capturing immediate advantages in your life, and the lives of others, using the power you already possess.

So forge onward. Speed through this compact manifesto with enthusiasm and purpose. Leave no page unread, and waste no time in reaching the end...

The Big Fucking Secret

And remember...
Life if just a ride...
<u>Enjoy every last moment</u>!

Eli Rook

The Big Fucking Secret

CHAPTER 1

Existence is comprised of gravity, mass, energy, and consciousness.

All physical matter is really just energy and mass, assembled in an endless field of gravity and consciousness.

Consciousness is the controlling component of existence.

You are consciousness.

You are the controller of existence.

You are God.

Zoom down beneath the smallest particle and there you are! Zoom out to view the widest multiverse and there you are again! You are consciousness. Your existence is eternal, all encompassing, and omnipresent.

•••

Consciousness has always existed.

Existence has always existed.

Consciousness *controls* existence.

You are consciousness.

You are the eternal conscious controller of existence.

Conscious Beings Are God.

The Big Fucking Secret

Never has there been a time when consciousness did not exist. And just the same, since you became conscious, there has never been a time when you haven't had the power to consciously control existence.

But there was a time when you were not *fully* conscious, and you did not *consciously* control existence... When you first took physical form in your current physical body you were not conscious... You were merely *spirit*.

You were a protoplasm, a product of nature. You were a highly intelligent animal with no consciousness whatsoever. You were smart, but not conscious. You only reacted to the world around you and exhibited no conscious characteristics whatsoever.

Later, after assimilating with other human beings on planet earth, you became conscious. You became God.

Your ability to use language accelerated. You assumed the capacity for reflective introspection. You were able to begin using consciousness tools, such as metaphors and analog models, assisting you in your ability to *access* consciousness.

Just as you became conscious of your self in your fresh new body, you developed a conscious awareness of your interface with all that "surrounds" you.

You also developed a conscious awareness of the interactions you held among other conscious beings you were "surrounded" by.

20

Although other conscious beings held a conscious awareness of you, they were surely convinced they were not God, and dually convinced *you too* were not God.

During the proceeding years, you learned from individuals who were confused about their role in the multiverse, and you observed their irrational assumptions about how reality works.

Eventually, for various reasons unique to your own individual experience, you rejected the fact that you are God, and you went on to live most of your life unaware of the fact that you control existence.

Luckily, one thing led to another and you decided you wanted to learn more about how this conscious life experience is conducted via your own individual management of personal intention.

You discovered how every quantum event is orchestrated based on your own personal fears and desires, and how all that "surrounds" you is really just a reflection of your internal customization of the existence field.

The Big Fucking Secret

This current moment is a reflection of an intention you held to have more, do more, or be more, and just like all of the other moments in your life, it's part of a sweeping movement in the eternal cosmic symphony you conduct as a conscious being.

Prior to this moment, you created an entire lifetime of situations and circumstances that led you here, where you now openly absorb the words in this book... reminding you of who you really are. *Life could have turned out differently - but it didn't!*

Instead of spending a lifetime actively navigating millions of situations and circumstances resulting in the discovery of a less accurate book, you orchestrated an entire lifetime of events yielding THIS book (which is the exact book you need to read RIGHT NOW to get more of what you want!)

See! You're a genius!

You DO control existence.

Consciousness controls time and space, reorganizing countless quantum events, so the most precise delivery of your deepest fears and desires are achieved, while the manifestation of your thoughts *renders* right before your very eyes – in real time...

And your constant awareness and enthusiasm about this fact takes you into greater symmetry with who you were meant to be. The fact that you're manifesting the experience of possessing this book, and the advantages you'll possess upon grasping its contents, is *just a taste* of what's possible once you acquire the power-harnessing perspectives revealed in the following chapters.

Eli Rook

Harnessing the power you've always held and using it to control the existence field in your favor begins with your acknowledgment of the fundamental concept expressed again and again throughout these pages...

You hold 100% control of everything you experience. *(Not 99%... Not 99.999%...)*

100%!!!

But you've experienced situations, circumstances, and events in the past during which you blamed external forces, and the actions of other conscious beings for the life experiences you've encountered.

This is because you were convinced that you did not personally hold 100% responsibility for those situations, circumstances, or events... You didn't acknowledge that you were 100% responsible for their manifestation.

That rejection of responsibility is the key factor in your life the authors of this book wish to help you vanish.

Upon vanishing the habit you've acquired to dismiss the fact that you are God, you're enabled to permanently ascend into the Civilization of Luminiferous Ascension, where you constantly feel the power of each event in your life serving the ultimate benefit of yourself and others.

While this is accomplished through constant effort and unwavering discipline, gaining access to that state of being is not dependent on any external force, other being, or milestone transformations in politics, business, intelligence, or society.

The Big Fucking Secret

It is not accomplished by reaching some far-off destination contingent on tipping points, shifts, revolutions, or "awakenings".

The awareness of your true nature is something you voluntarily step into RIGHT NOW, and the transformation of the world around you, as it bends to your will, is a phenomenon in perpetual motion.

You are God RIGHT NOW, and you always have been since your initiation into consciousness. Being the controller of existence is your evolved nature. (It is the evolved nature of ALL conscious beings.)

Your HABITUAL AWARENESS of who you *really* are is the foundation upon which you endlessly pursue becoming more of who you deserve to become.

As you endeavor to consume the pages of this book you'll acquire a widening understanding of this foundational concept and work toward developing the habitual awareness of "being God".

Then, you'll go on to learn beyond what's taught in the pages of this book by using your own life experience as a *far superior* source of enlightenment.

You're here for one of two reasons...

Eli Rook

You're either keen on forging progress to establish a new world in which you can thrive, or you're already working in harmony with the silent heroes of civilization to bring forth its manifestation.

Those who are already aware of the fact that they are God control existence in their favor to the increasing benefit of family, friends, community, and society in general.

We work in almost every industry and have a variety of economic, religious, philosophical, and ancestral backgrounds. But we hold one thing in common that binds us together...

We Are Consumed With A Passion For Creating Success

We understand at the core of our being exists a multiversal singularity.

That singularity is expressed through the art we create, the business we conduct, and the breakthroughs in new knowledge we produce.

That singularity with "The All" is the pulsation of <u>pure love</u> and <u>integrated honesty</u>. It guides us toward an ever-increasing symmetry with new world quantum trajectories void of crime, disease, poverty, death, and all that's in contradiction with the nature of evolved conscious beings.

The Big Fucking Secret

This consciously controlled love-singularity is manifesting monumental transitions all around planet Earth, as you can easily observe:

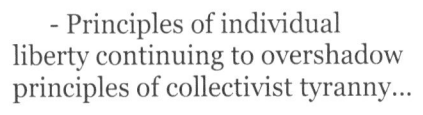

- Principles of individual liberty continuing to overshadow principles of collectivist tyranny...

- Holistic healing solutions rising to overshadow medical industry manipulations...

- Alternative currencies positioned to outcompete government-abused fiat currencies...

- And independent entrepreneurial drive outshining grumpy, dead-end, routine-rut "jobs".

You see the results of our benevolent power manifesting all around you. (You've personally been effected in ways you might not even acknowledge.)

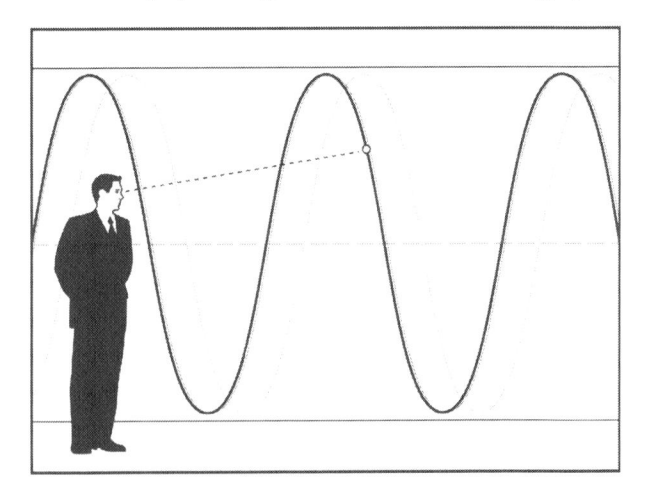

Eli Rook

Just look at how this planet has been transformed over the last one hundred years.

In modernized countries there are libraries in every town. Anyone who wants to read and write can easily find free instruction, support, and encouragement.

Drinkable running water flows freely in public places, and inexpensively into the homes of all those who inhabit the developed world.

Electricity is affordable and available in abundance. Hot water, refrigeration, and electrically-heated cooking devices are a luxury taken for granted.

Transportation is affordable and more available than ever before. Virtually anyone can travel thousands of miles quickly and inexpensively. Cheap, dependable, used automobiles are in excess on every continent.

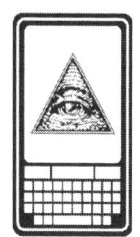

Instantaneous global communications are dirt cheap and prices continue to plummet.

Affordable pocket-sized devices enable individuals to access all public digital information on planet Earth from any location a service signal can be found.

The start-up cost for someone to begin generating financial capital operating an internet-based business is virtually zero, and opportunities are in abundance regardless of physical location.

The Big Fucking Secret

A wide selection of self-organized social organizations, clubs, and societies exist in which any individual can quickly assimilate into a new community and build mutually beneficial relationships.

While there are inevitable production challenges to be endured, food is in abundance throughout the modern world and thousands of brilliant minds are working diligently to confront supply issues in the face of population growth and resource depletion.

Technologies and information enabling individuals to enjoy vibrant dynamic health are accessible to all, and natural health practitioners are more accessible than ever before.

Late in the first decade of the 21st century, a tipping point was reached where the number of individuals in America who claim to support a particular political party was SUPERCEDED by the number of individuals aware of the banker-controlled two-party hoax.

In the second decade of the 21st century, criminal political systems around the world gasp for their last breath, similar to how superstitious religions gasped for their last breath in the decade prior.

Eli Rook
We Truly Are Living In A New World Order.

The perspective an individual has about the condition of the world around them is certainly a reflection of the health in which they view their own existence.

One can view the world around them in apocalyptic decline toward Armageddon, or... One can view the world around them in a <u>transitional</u> <u>state</u> *(experiencing some minor growing pains)* while understanding a variety of means will ensure its return to vibrant health.

If your perspective of life on Earth is one of immense possibility, motivated enthusiasm, and eager anticipation, this book can offer like-minded perspectives that help render the Civilization of Luminiferous Ascension in your life experience with greater speed.

But if your perspective of life on Earth is dismal and dreary, perhaps this book can offer a glimpse of what lies beyond the storm cloud... What those of us who enjoy the illumination of the new world clearly see.

The Big Fucking Secret

Ultimately, you'll be the final judge of whether or not your perspectives are healthy for you – so consider this...

You were once a resident in the Civilization of Luminiferous Ascension ...And if it's your desire to return – regardless of your age, or location – you certainly may...

It's only a decision away.

The child of your past, who loved every moment of life and all its wonders, is still inside you... Eager to be set free... Eager to once again command the cosmos for pleasure and profit, to the benefit of nature, and every other conscious being in existence.

That child of the past wishes for nothing more than to live every last moment CONSUMED WITH LOVE, basking in the endless potentiality of The All – enjoying the natural exhilaration of life!

Let's begin to retrace our steps and understand what happened to that child all those years ago, back before you were convinced that you were not God...

Eli Rook

The Big Fucking Secret

CHAPTER 2

Existence is comprised of mass, energy, and consciousness inside super inflated gravity units.

Everything you see, hear, smell, taste, touch – and everything you perceive *beyond* the five senses - is ultimately energy, mass, gravity, and consciousness.

While gravity units make up the foundation of all existence, energy, mass, and consciousness are its core components. (Consciousness is the controlling component.)

You are a conscious being.

Conscious beings control existence.

Conscious beings are God.

You exist within multiple dimensions of existence. This multidimensional matrix yields endless potentiality and limitless combinations of situations and circumstances to be controlled by conscious beings.

Conscious beings control what "is" (otherwise known as reality) by customizing individual life experience within the matrix.

You are a multidimensional conscious being in control of reality; controlling existence.

You are God.

The Big Fucking Secret

**Existence and reality have
no beginning and no end.**

Contrary to popular new age cliches, you do not *create* reality... nor do you create existence (just as you do not create the laws of physics).

(Reality could never have been created because it never existed in a state where it did not exist.)

Energy, consciousness, gravity, and mass cannot be created, nor can they be destroyed, thus reality is a dynamic vortex of limitless possibilities, existing eternally, created by no one, "collectively" controlled by all conscious beings.

The unique collection of experiences throughout your past, your present, and your future - both to your liking and to your dismay - are customized by YOU, alongside each conscious being within the multidimensional matrix of existence. *(A "life experience" is the streaming assembly of postulates manifest by the Pulsation of an individual, their contemporaries, and intelligences yet to be identified - All of which are God).*

While you do not create reality, you do <u>conduct</u> a unique individual experience within reality. You possess the innate capacity as a conscious being to hold 100% conscious control over the unique experience you conduct, which could loosely be referred to as "your reality". This includes the manner in which you traverse the "intersecting" life experiences of other conscious beings.

Eli Rook

Your individual life experience is optimally rendered based on the <u>pulsation of energy</u> you emit...

All of the events, as well as all the conscious beings co-existing with you throughout the multidimensional matrix, are <u>dynamically</u> and <u>perpetually</u> <u>customized</u> to match your Pulsation, as your life experience renders.

From an omnidimensional perspective, each conscious being exists in an *endless array* of potential quantum "positions", and the rendering of each specific quantum "position" other conscious beings conduct into your life experience, is completely unique to you – *drawn forth to best match your pulsation of energy*.

In a similar fashion, the quantum positions you conduct into the life experiences of other conscious beings are equally unique to them – rendering to best match the individual pulsations of energy *they* emit.

Your Pulsation customizes the ENTIRE WORLD rendering in your life experience. It's completely unique to you, and completely under your control.

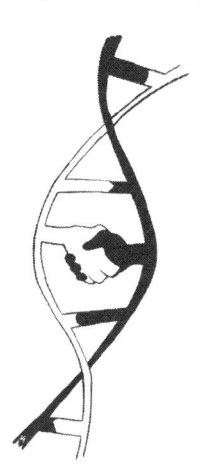

Ultimately, each conscious being consciously controls the ever-changing, multidimensional holographic renderings of events transpiring throughout the existence field, including the intersecting life experiences of other conscious beings.

While you explore this rabbit hole of multidimensional complexity, be mindful of the basic idea that ALL you experience is being optimally rendered in a capacity completely unique to you. (We will simplify and expand upon this principle as we proceed.)

The Big Fucking Secret
Let's review the functionality of your manifestation technology.

In your current biological form you possess a mind, a brain, and a body. The biological form you've assumed is an integrated unit which conducts the energy of conscious and unconscious thoughts.

Your thoughts are energetic in nature, and oscillate as vibrational waveform frequencies, called brainwaves, which are emitted from the brain into the etheric field, the matrix, the multiverse, or the 10th dimension (what this book shall refer to as "The All").

These frequencies (information, vibrations, energies, etc,) are emitted from the brain similar to the way radio wave frequencies are transmitted from a radio tower, with the distinction that thoughts, when transmitted from the brain, actually permeate the ENTIRE existence field instantaneously.

This instantaneous permeation of The All by the constant stream of frequencies you're emitting with each new unit of thought, could more aptly be compared to how a light bulb instantaneously permeates the entire room with light when a lamp is turned on[1].

While you transmit your stream of thoughts into existence, you're instantaneously filling the entire existence field with each new thought, whether you like it or not.

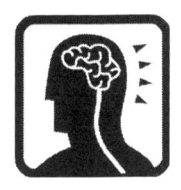

---

[1] Note in the lamp analogy that light (photons) can only shine so far and travel so fast. Your thoughts on the other hand instantaneously permeate the ENTIRE existence field without any loss of intensity.

Eli Rook

The existence field is endless in size and it holds all the thoughts from all the conscious beings who ever thought a thought.

All of the thoughts from all the conscious beings who ever thought a thought – including you – and all the new thoughts emitted as each moment passes, effect all the physical matter in existence.

On the most fundamental quantum level, your thoughts (and all the thoughts of all the other conscious beings) are interacting with EVERYTHING - the air you breathe, the furniture lining the space in which you reside, the trees and the dirt covering the planet you inhabit, the star you're orbiting around, and beyond.

Your thoughts are woven throughout EVERYTHING, permeating the endless field of existence in which you exist.

You're also "processing".

Your brain has the capability of *receiving* all the frequencies emitted by all the other brains right now, as well as the frequencies emitted by all the other brains that ever existed, *and will ever exist into the future*.

You're transmitting and receiving THOUGHTS (waveform frequencies, or information), like an eternal, omnipresent, multidimensional walkie talkie. All the while, your thoughts are effecting The All, shaping, and molding physical matter (mass and energy) in ways which best adhere to your stream of thought, contributing to everything that renders in your individual life experience.

The Big Fucking Secret

The All efficiently yields situations and circumstances that you constantly encounter as your life experience persists, and you control The All with your "Pulsation".

Your Pulsation is comprised of two unique components: "The sum of your thoughts" (which includes what you consciously and unconsciously process in the mind and brain), and the vibration of your DNA.

Ultimately, at any given moment, you're pulsating the sum of your *fears*, your *desires*, and you biological state.

The situations and circumstances you encounter throughout your life experience are customized and governed by your pulsation of energy, and your constant awareness of this fact enables you to gain more conscious control over how your life experience will transpire.

Consider the space you're in right now as a structure of energy, mass, and gravity configured to be a perfect match to your Pulsation. You're EXACTLY where you need to be right now based on everything you aspire to be, everything you fear, and all you are biologically.

Your friends are a rendering of quantum particles delivering the most precise interactions to match your Pulsation. They're the perfect custom made friends based on everything you aspire to be, everything you fear and all you are biologically.

Eli Rook

The information you've had access to, the information you're currently absorbing, and all the information you'll soon have access to, is all materializing on a precision time track based on what you need to know and when you need to know it, as commanded by your Pulsation.

You've probably heard the saying, "When the student is ready, the teacher will appear..." It's true - and it's no mystery why you're learning what you're learning RIGHT NOW!

Each subsequent moment is custom built (by you) so you may encounter the experiences necessary to further render your deepest fears & desires, and affect the degree in which you biologically evolve outside of nature.

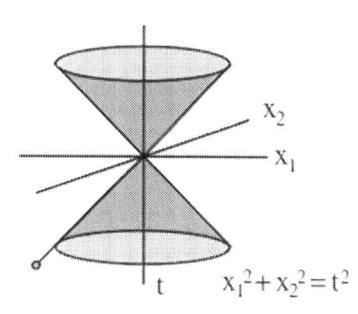

You exist in a perpetual vortex of organized existence where your pulsation programs the spacetime coordinates of every quantum event as they relate to your unique life experience.

$$x_1^2 + x_2^2 = t^2$$

You thoughts are at the forefront of such phenomena...

This was popularly communicated in the "The Strangest Secret", by Earl Nightingale, which became the best selling self-development recording in history.

Simply put, The Strangest Secret is: *"You become (or you get) what you think about most of the time."*

39

The Big Fucking Secret

Prior to "The Strangest Secret", the phenomenon was popularly described in a book titled "Think and Grow Rich", by Napoleon Hill, who is regarded by many as the most influential author in history on the subject of success. Hill famously proposed, *"Whatever the mind of man can conceive and bring itself to be believe, it can achieve."*

And prior to that, a gentleman named Wallace D. Wattles wrote in his landmark publication The Science of Getting Rich *"There's a thinking stuff from which all things are made, and which, in its original state, permeates, penetrates, and fills the interspaces of the universe."*

The same idea echoes throughout countless religious and occult texts produced by various cultures throughout history on planet Earth, and the clarity of this idea is growing at a rapid pace in the minds of conscious beings conducting intersecting life experiences with your own.

For decades scientists have increasingly proven the validity of these ideas and more recently, popular films like "What The Bleep Do We Know?" and "The Secret" attempt to present the modern proofs offered by quantum mechanics research for mass consumption.

Upon this book's latest publication, a nonstop explosion of breakthrough scientific research exploring how consciousness controls existence increasingly thunders through the mainstream establishment[2].

---

[2] Mounting evidence of a "God Particle" uncovered by research scientists at the CERN Institute in Switzerland came to the forefront of global scientific acclaim in July 2012, and new discoveries in this field will continuously mount in the coming years and decades leading up to The Singularity .

Eli Rook

As you become increasingly conscious of the fact that you are God and conscious of how "the strangest secret" has been in play throughout your entire life, you assemble the puzzle pieces that form an illustrated picture depicting your life-long control of existence.

With the cognition that you control how your individual experience is rendered, you can look back and see, with greater clarity, how you've used your power to form and mold everything you've experienced throughout your life.

The Strangest Secret becomes less and less strange as you experience the cognition of it's phenomenon, and as more and more conscious individuals experience the cognition alongside yourself, it seems to become *less and less of a secret!*

Isn't it peculiar how information just comes to you; how books virtually jump off the shelf into your hands!?

Isn't it funny how you meet the exact individual you need to meet when you're trying to accomplish a task, or create a specific outcome?

And isn't it funny how nothing goes your way when you're feeling bad, smoldering in a heap of rotten victimized thoughts?

Not really...

The Big Fucking Secret

You control existence and existence reflects what you think about most of the time. *Existence is reflection of your Pulsation.*

Your Pulsation bends, molds, and sculpts The All - customizing your life experience from the complete spectrum of potential situations, circumstances, and events available to you.

Now that you understand how this works you'll want to play around with the power you're harnessing and use it to consciously control what you experience in the future... Right?

Perhaps you want to live debt-free and enjoy all of your needs being met for the rest of your life...

You can do it!

Perhaps you want deeper relationships with family, friends, and your partner(s)...

You can have it!

Maybe you want more power in transforming your community, or your planet, so other individuals can come into more awareness of the fact that they too control existence.

It's All Happening
<u>RIGHT NOW!</u>

(The possibilities are endless.)

You are the conductor. Your thoughts are pulsating and permeating The All moment by moment, effecting all the physical matter in existence, bending and molding existence to your will.

Your brain is a quantum computer instantly receiving and processing all the information in existence, and you're increasingly harnessing its awesome power to command forth all the experiences you desire.

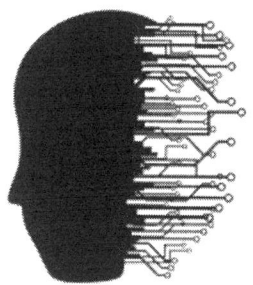

With these realizations, do you intend to use all your power to draw forth a life experience delivering *more happiness*, *more wealth*, *better health*, *fulfilling relationships*, and virtually ANYTHING else you want?

...*Of course you do!*

Let's dive in...

The Big Fucking Secret

CHAPTER 3

While conscious beings control the existence field to manifest unique individual life experiences, incomplete ideas about reality are continuously encountered.

As one fills in the puzzle pieces to complete these ideas, a conceptualization of The All grows in complexity.

And with the increasing complexity of one's understanding of The All, incomplete ideas form anew.

Thus, a conscious beings is in the perpetual process of actively completing incomplete ideas – or *integrating knowledge* – as their life experience persists.

The degree of skill in which you may consciously control reality to your favor correlates with the degree of honesty in which you integrate knowledge.

The journey toward symmetry you've achieved as a conscious being thus far has primarily been accomplished by the degree of accuracy in which you've integrated all the knowledge you've acquired.

The Big Fucking Secret was tactically crafted to help you achieve wider integrations of knowledge and accelerate toward the speed and quality of integration possessed by those who consciously control existence to their favor on planet Earth.

The Big Fucking Secret

Knowledge possessed but not integrated is knowledge not yet used, and your drift away from symmetry is partly a result of possessing knowledge not yet used...

But more significantly, knowledge obtained and *dishonestly* integrated yields a mythology which persists in the absence of integrated honesty – resulting in a conceptual "simulation" of reality to be experienced.

ya Got Trouble! *Any actions put forth in "simulation mode" ultimately become fruitless, counterproductive, even physically destructive.*

As an innocent child you acquired knowledge about reality in an attempt to understand who you were, what you were meant to do, and the role conscious beings play throughout the existence field.

You may have developed mythology while failing to accurately integrate knowledge, and established a simulated conceptualization of how reality works. If so, this would have caused you to unknowingly occupy a life trajectory apart from the core path to become who you were meant to be.

The most common (and subsequently the most damaging) mythology obtained in "simulation mode" is the idea that God exists outside of you, separate from you: up in the sky, out there, unreachable, externally authoritative – "someone" to whom you were subservient.

Eli Rook

You may have concluded that "God" was an external authority having absolute control over the lives of conscious beings, like a heavenly zookeeper forever cleaning out the cages of savage, incompetent mortals.

Regardless of the wide variety of wacky mythology you may have developed, you were most certainly convinced at times you did not have 100% control over everything that transpired in your life.

You were largely convinced outside forces ultimately determined most of what happened in your life, and you were simply a vessel experiencing whatever the universe, nature, society, and "God" happened to throw in your face.

Even in your most valiant attempts to establish an atheistic view, you were still a ship lost out at sea, drifting hither and thither in the winds of time; your fate sealed by random causality...

NOT ANYMORE!

In the fog of mythological simulations, the organization of your thoughts and actions yielded but a small sampling of life experiences that were symmetrical with the core path toward who you were meant to be.

You have at many times tasted the sweet nectar of your eternal omnipresence and your vast command of cosmic energy, experiencing the rush of powerful a-ha moments, the sensory explosion of an earth-shaking orgasm, or the impenetrable strength and confidence of being RECOGNIZED as a champion.

The Big Fucking Secret

While you had achieved a profound symmetry in those fleeting moments of larger-than-life control, you eventually found yourself back in the distorted perception of a mortal body, facing fear of annihilation by the inevitable wrath of man, society, "God", government, or whatever external force you elected to rule over you.

You have the power to vanquish the mythologies which prohibit your favorable command of reality…

And the foremost mythology, which has been at the root of ALL your misfortune, and ALL your unfavorable experiences, is the erroneous conceptualization that you are not in TOTAL control of everything you experience in life.

Your existence-controlling nature as a conscious being is something you are irrevocably bound to – it is *who you are* and *what you are*. You are at the source of EVERYTHING you experience; both favorable and unfavorable. It is the essence of your being.

If you herd around the planet alongside your fellow mortals, possessing a deeply ingrained, and deceptively convincing mythology that your entire life experience is being dictated by outside forces, your overall well-being and happiness in life will certainly be degraded.

But upon integrating the realization that you are God, you identify the perceptions and conceptualizations you held in the past as being the metaphysical shackles restraining you in a subjective old world of guaranteed peril.

As you widen your ability to identify the experiences throughout your life which occurred as a direct result of your failure to take 100% responsibility as the controller of existence, you begin to have cognitions and realizations about your command over "outside influences" you've come to encounter.

Clarity about your true power unfolds and an awareness of your control in the present moment springs forth so the new-world-perspective you begin to encounter induces your quantum crossing into a fifth dimensional orientation with reality.

Upon experiencing a sufficient number of quantum crossings you suddenly find yourself in a new world looking back, as opposed to where you previously were, blindfolded in the old world, at the behest of your mythologies.

Take a look back at some perspectives from the old world... Think about how reality controlled you the whole time you were convinced that you were not God, and how you perceived a host of outside influences and external forces controlling the direction of your life's course.

The Big Fucking Secret

For instance, you at one time considered the government controlled what you could or couldn't do...

Knowing what you know now, it seems ridiculous to think that you were NOT a sovereign citizen of the universe, owing duty to an irrational structure of false authority.

Like so many others before the internet age, you may have considered that local and global economies, as well as your formal education, ultimately controlled how much money you could make – and the limited ways you could spend it.

Until recently, populations of the world decided their ability to experience fine food, international travel, fashionable clothing, and premium transportation depended on how the job market fared, and what type of institutional credentials they possessed.

For nearly 40 years, many individuals living in North America believed an ineffective healthcare system was responsible for controlling how long they lived, and the quality of life they could experience!

They thought they needed to see medical doctors and take pharmaceutical drugs in order to stay happy and healthy!

For centuries, billions of conscious beings thought that words in a book, and the spokespeople of religions controlled what they could believe, how they could think, and who they could fuck!

A retardation of conscious thought and emotional freedom manifested by billions of people who were convinced they were not God made for a very interesting account of history.

If it wasn't the government, the economy, the educational system, the healthcare system, or zany religions that controlled what you could be, do, or have, you may have believed some other outside influence was responsible for your drift away from symmetry: your parents, your spouse, your children, your pets, your horoscope, your body, the weather, society, karma, or any number of external things.

We now SHIFT AWAY from the ILLUSION that outside forces control us!

Since you reached a point in your existence where you acknowledge there are NO OUSIDE INFLUENCES that control you - *and YOU are the only one holding the power to live the life you were meant to live*, the existence field is currently filling your life experience with an abundance of circumstances and situations set to transpire for the sole purpose of enabling you to manifest ALL the core-path-compatible dreams and desires you've ever held!

The Big Fucking Secret

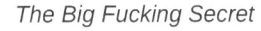

In these early stages of your initial efforts to take 100% responsibility for everything that happens in your life, you may question the fact that you're the controller of existence, and attempt to rationalize how outside influences actually DO effect you...

This is because you developed a deeply ingrained habit of living in your own mythology. The habit is typified by rationalizations that reject self-responsibility, and a resistance to integrating knowledge you've already acquired *(namely the knowledge that you are God, and you hold responsibility for everything you experience)*.

For instance, you may propose an observation such as, "I got stuck in traffic this morning. How is that my fault, and not the fault of the other drivers?"

You raise your consciousness by understanding you, and only you, controlled what time you got out of bed, and what time you left the house... You controlled the circumstances of how fast or slow you were traveling, and your responsibility for identifying opportunities to access the fastest, shortest routes.

You actually controlled COUNTLESS other factors going all the way back to the day before, and the day before that - *all the way back to the beginning of your life* - all accumulating to place you in the precise situation you found yourself in.

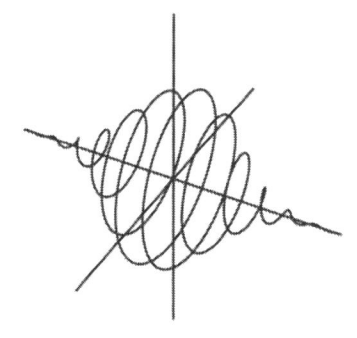

EVERYTHING, whether it be favorable or not, is all 100% under your control and absolutely NO outside influences can be blamed or credited.

You are part of The All and you are ONE with The All... You're responsible for everything that happened throughout your ENTIRE life experience, because everything that happened throughout your life experience was a manifestation of your thoughts and actions!

In the old world, under your old world mythology, you might claim Exo-God to be at fault...

But in the new world you can understand what it's like being in total control while you're conscious of the fact that you are God - and NOT being in total control when you doubt or discredit such a fact.

You can understand how everything happening right now is a result of time spent controlling reality to manifest that which is in your favor, as well as time spent controlling reality to manifest that which is not.

Moving forward, improving your ability to take 100% responsibility for everything you experience in life, you go on to encounter fluctuations of observable, measurable results - mounting perhaps slowly at first, then with increasing speed - until dawn breaks over the horizon and you begin consciously controlling reality - navigating the situations and circumstances you experience with grace... the favorable outcomes you desire *magically transpiring* right before your eyes.

The Big Fucking Secret

Your ascension into a fifth dimensional orientation with reality is a symphony of challenges overcome, stretching onward toward a destination in time unknown prior to your arrival.

Constant effort, error, and correction improve the efficacy of your control, further disengaging your old self-imposed sentence in the prisoner paradigm, unshackling you from a self-imposed limitation of fourth dimensional conscious orientation.

Eventually, as you continue to proceed in such a manner, you'll increasingly notice more and more conscious beings conducting life in a similar sport.

This is because, unbeknownst to you, everything you perceive ultimately reflects that which you have become thus far in your life experience.

And now that you've been inducted into this new paradigm of thought, as your quantum triangulation shifts, you will eventually find those around you subtly following suit.

Eli Rook

The Big Fucking Secret

CHAPTER 4

Throughout your life, the sum of your conscious and unconscious thoughts, including all that you fear, and all that you desire, has pulsated an uninterrupted command into the existence field, dynamically customizing your ongoing conscious experience.

You've been conducting power throughout the entire realm of existence entangled with your life experience – *throughout your entire conscious existence* – even during instances where your power manifested unfavorable circumstances you may have erroneously deemed out of your control.

You have always been the CONDUCTOR...

And the power has always been on... (You're the only one who conducts the current flowing into your life.)

Every conscious being has the innate power to *consciously conduct* a life experience full of prosperity, health, and security – without difficulty, struggle, or hardship. And every conscious being endures a learning process to acquire *illumination* in understanding this innate power.

Illumination is acquired through a perpetual engagement in understanding the innate power we all possess, while exerting effort to conduct that power into the fulfillment of one's *life purpose*; to experience happiness, and serve other conscious beings to better fulfill their life purpose.

The Big Fucking Secret

The Big Fucking Secret will guide you in conducting the grand symphony of your control over existence down to a singular note on the sheet music standing before you.

First, you'll *clearly* define a specific desire or outcome that is currently available to you within the realm of *potentiality...*

Your specific desire will have an overwhelming & conclusive objective probability that dictates it not only can manifest, but ultimately WILL manifest.

(This one single desire must be charged with a seeming destiny. It must be so ripe, so appealing, and so heavily magnetized to you that it becomes part of you – it is conducted in a manner of certainty.)

Then, you'll apply constant effort – e*xerting concentrated thought and action* – to program the existence field so your desire renders into your life experience.

With practice, as you gain confidence and power from achieving a stream of consistent, favorable results, you'll eventually manage to conduct your desires into your experience at will, instantly rendering them on "auto-pilot".

But before we cover the technical details of defining specific desires and programing the field, we'll briefly review how the mind, brain, and body work, and how your interface with the multidimensional matrix to conduct potentiality into actuality.

The physical body contains organs, muscles, bones, fluid, cartilage, tendons, and electrical wiring. Energy flows through the body powering its ability to perform physical actions and capture sensory stimulation.

The body is an electromagnetic circuit and construct for your residual self image.

The brain is housed inside the body and controls the body. Not only is the brain a transmitter broadcasting brainwaves that instantaneously permeate The All, but it's also responsible for generating, managing, and distributing electricity throughout the body. It runs the nervous system, circulatory systems, muscles, and organs – and produces a host of chemical reactions – all without any *conscious* effort.

The brain is an electrical power station and analog quantum computer.

The mind, which surrounds and permeates the body, is typically referred to as one's electromagnetic field, aura, etc. It's the utility in which individual human beings on planet Earth *access* consciousness[3].

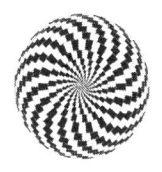

The mind is a digital processor of multidimensional information.

The mind controls the brain, the brain controls the body, and you control the mind... (because you are God).

---

[3] Individual consciousness is not part of nature's automatic operating system. Consciousness is the omnipresent controlling component of existence, *harnessed* by individual conscious beings in order to control nature.

The Big Fucking Secret

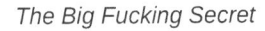

When you are not conscious of the fact that you are God, you allow your brain, body, and mind to run partly by way of nature's automatic operating system, which is ever-present, forcing nature's evolutionary survival pressures upon your physiological makeup. When you use your mind to be conscious of the fact that you are God, you may override nature's automatic operating system, gaining conscious control of the mind, brain, body, AND The All (as well as your own evolution).

When you are not conscious of the fact that you are God, you are subject to inevitably perilous external influences and outside forces, such as other conscious beings, and nature itself. *(When you are fully conscious of the fact that you are God and you're taking 100% responsibility for your life, outside influences do not effect you in such a manner.)*

You, God, are conscious of your housing within the body, and you're conscious of the mind surrounding and permeating the body. You're conscious of the brain inside the body and you're becoming increasingly conscious of your integral role within The All[4]. But when you are convinced that you are not God, you DEVOLVE into a somewhat helpless automaton of nature.

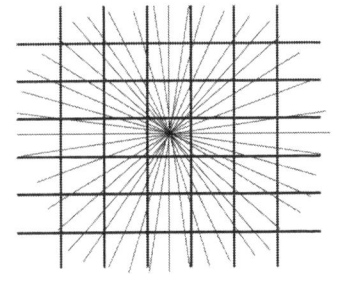

---

[4] Your role within The All (your purpose for living) is to experience happiness and be a benefactor to other conscious beings, by creating success. *(Success is the progressive manifestation of a predestined desire.)*

Eli Rook

The All consists of multiple dimensions of existence.

The first dimension consists of a single line between two points, and the second dimension consists of a set of intersecting lines.

Examples of two-dimensional existence include grids, waveforms, as well as flat geometric shapes.

In the third dimension, "flat" intersecting lines of the second dimension "stretch" into third dimensional points.

For example, first imagine a one-dimensional line...

Next, imagine four of those lines being connected to assemble a flat two-dimensional square.

Now imagine a third-dimensional point above the square...

If you draw four lines starting from the third-dimensional point, down to each individual corner of the square, you'd complete the formation of a PYRAMID.

Simply put, the third dimension consists of specific configurations in which first and second dimensional existence "stretch" into third dimensional points, to form third dimensional existence.

The *fourth dimension* is the continuous "folding" of a three-dimensional state into another, enabling third dimensional existence to persist in a *transitory fashion*.

The changing nature of fourth dimensional existence is conceptually observed as TIME passing by.

The Big Fucking Secret

Imagine within the fourth dimension, the third dimension is constantly "updating" from one "state" into the next... *(Right now, observable existence is in one state... And a moment later it's in another!)*

Observable existence from a fourth dimensional orientation *changes* as time passes. But what exactly determines HOW it will change next? What determines each subsequent fourth dimensional "event", as each changing moment transpires?

The fifth dimension consists of an endless number of potential fourth dimensional events.

A fifth dimensional postulate is any "future" event adhering to the laws of physics, dependent on everything that's occurred up until now.

Third dimensional states (static) *combine* to form "strings" of fourth dimensional events (transitory), which are *selected* from the fifth dimension (dynamic), and *rendered* in your multidimensional life experience.

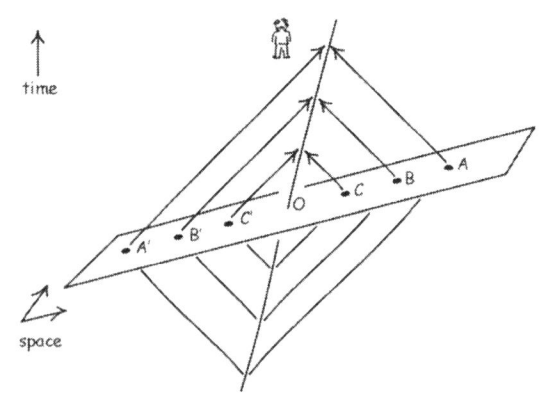

<u>YOU ARE THE ONE</u> commanding the realm of fifth dimensional potentiality to render as the unique life experience you conduct persists!

Conscious beings on Earth control reality by commanding fifth dimensional postulates to flow into their life experience.

Conscious beings are God!

Conscious beings are voluntarily connected to the The All, conducting power to control the vortex of multidimensional existence.

Endless fifth dimensional postulates are intentionally and contiguously rendered into the unique individual life experiences of every conscious being.

The unique individual life experiences conducted by other conscious beings holographically intersect your own in the most optimum capacity, based on the pulsation of energy you emit from the specific quantum position you endure within the vortex.

You sprung forth from nature to acquire the capacity in which you harnessed multidimensional consciousness, and you reached the brink of fifth dimensional conscious orientation. You then acquired the disease of the mind, after which your perception of reality was demoted to a fourth dimensional orientation, fostering an illusion that you were controlled by the external force of nature, "Exo-God", government, other conscious beings, etc.

The Big Fucking Secret

But now you're engaged in quantum crossings into a fifth dimensional orientation with reality, curing the disease of the mind, and using your power to move into a quantum trajectory that holds symmetry with who you are meant to be.

To acquire a fifth dimensional orientation, first ponder the fourth dimensional perspective of existence by observing the persistence of reality as time rolls forward. Observe the flowing symphony of each passing moment.

Then, contemplate a third dimensional perspective of existence as you observe a "snapshot" of the (seemingly) immobile solid matter all around you...

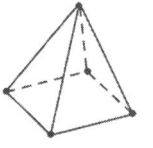

Next, deconstruct those third dimensional snapshots into a second dimensional perspective of existence, as you observe the flat interconnecting geometries that underlie the physical matter in those snapshots.

Now further venture to deconstruct the second dimension into a first dimensional perspective of existence as you observe the lines that extend to support those geometries.

Now observe the ubiquitous points underlying all that's constructed around you throughout the existence field!

Finally, observe how the points, lines, shapes, and physical matter all around you are woven throughout time as it passes by.

Eli Rook

Consider the fourth dimensional perspective of existence as a collection of static third dimensional states *transitioning* from one form into the next, like the frames in a reel of film as they're fed past the lens of a movie projector.

Now, observe the FIFTH dimensional perspective of reality as a vast realm of ENDLESS POTENTIALITY streaming into your life experience... *your imagination sifting and sorting all that potentiality into the present moment, which then flows into the next.*

As you encounter each moment, existence is being formed and molded to incorporate the fifth dimensional options you've consciously and unconsciously selected, and your pulsation of energy is constantly programming the multidimensional matrix of existence to render, with perfection, the precise life experience you command.

(You are a powerful multidimensional conscious being programming The All, controlling existence from moment to moment, as each tiny moment passes...)

The All is your playground where you command forth all that you fear and all that you desire from all-that-is-possible.

All-that-is-possible includes everything favorable and everything not so favorable... Everything that causes life to flourish, and everything which causes life to diminish.

ll-that-is-possible means ANYTHING CAN HAPPEN, with regard to all that has passed, the laws of physics, and the creative capacity of conscious beings.

The Big Fucking Secret

The fifth dimension holds endless potential for abundance and scarcity at the behest of God.

God permeates and governs The All, and there is no higher power than the power of conscious beings... The power of God.

We are all woven into the eternal, fractalized, luminiferous pulsation of existence, commanding potentiality from all-there-could-be to organize itself in all-there-is-right-now, and all-there-will-be as life persists...

Yet the realm of existence over which you reign is 100% administered by you, and 100% unique to you.

And it is a lack of illumination in this area of knowledge through which a mythology may fester...

When someone is convinced that they are not God, and encounters an experience which is deemed unfavorable, they proceed to blame outside influences and external forces as the reason why such an unfavorable experience occured.

Yet all along, every unfavorable experience is a perfect match to that conscious being's pulsation of energy, largely determined by the sum of their thoughts.

The All efficiently and courteously delivers situations and circumstances which are <u>perfectly</u> <u>matched</u> to the command of your pulsation. Your pulsation of energy is continuously programming The All to optimally draw forth 5th dimensional postulates holding a synchronistic kinship with all that you fear and all that you desire.

Eli Rook

The 5th dimension is neither benevolent nor malevolent. It's simply a "buffet" of endless potentiality open to your consumption, and your illumination in regard to this paradigm should provide a basis upon which all mythology may be eradicated.

Thus, your objective as a conscious multidimensional conductor of experience is to become fully conscious of the fact that you are God, and control existence to maximize your happiness, while best serving others. In doing so you not only illuminate yourself, but you illuminate the world – because the "world" is simply a rendering of your command over 5th dimensional potentiality.

This is optimally achieved through moving from a 4th dimensional conscious orientation within the existence field into a 5th dimensional orientation within the existence field, in effect curing the disease of the mind, and enabling eternal happiness, prosperity, and safety to permeate your experience.

Your permanent quantum crossing into a fifth dimensional orientation with reality is best sought through a passionate organized effort to enjoy consistent levels of extreme happiness while achieving success in manifesting your desires.

The core path to becoming *the-person-you-are-meant-to-be* is paved with your passionate drive to forge progress in manifesting desires that serve your best self-interest and the well-being of others, despite whatever discouraging problems "the world" might be facing.

The Big Fucking Secret

With progress being made, you are the light that shines forth upon the perceived darkness witnessed by any other conscious being whose life experience happens to intersect your own.

Enjoy the cognition of how the entire existence field is your personal playground, and look toward the fifth dimension of abundant potentiality with a grin...

The ascension to an unobstructed fifth dimensional orientation with reality is your final evolution into consciousness.

The endless buffet of options will always be at your command, and in the following chapters of this book you'll learn exactly how to identify 5th dimensional postulates and consciously "render" them in your life.

But first we'll explore the evolutionary leap out of the a pre-conscious past endured by our ancestors several millenia past.

Eli Rook

The Big Fucking Secret

CHAPTER 5

There is a "spirit" of life which permeates nature and constantly thrives as existence grows in complexity through the will of conscious beings.

With the concentration of spirit in a particular realm of existence, optimum conditions manifest where lifeforms gain the intelligence and biological complexity required to break free from nature's restrictive constraints.

Thousands of years ago, when human beings on planet Earth reached the boundaries of unconscious potentiality, the dull cumbersome limitations of nature's automatic operating system could no longer serve the accelerating demands for evolutionary advancement.

Thus, over time, the entire human species "leaped" into consciousness.

The spirit of humanity leaped forward into a new realm of *sophistication* and *harmony* with nature, taking control of its own evolutionary progress in order to thrive beyond the *automatic existence* of non-conscious life.

Humankind leaped into consciousness, assimilating into the *dynamic existence* of God, taking control of nature, for the betterment of all life.

Such phenomena continuously unfolds throughout the existence field: *Nature brings forth the conditions in which non-conscious life evolves... non-conscious life evolves to acquire cutting-edge intelligence... and highly intelligent lifeforms leap into consciousness, accelerating beyond the cutting edge of natural selection.*

Consciousness is the highest "power" in existence. It's the controlling force woven throughout all existence. It permeates existence and it's harnessed by lifeforms who evolve in sophistication to a degree in which consciousness becomes a necessity for their advancement.

Lifeforms harness consciousness to establish new conditions where the proliferation of conscious life may enrich the spiritual abundance which permeates nature.

Unfettered disease-free consciousness is initially harnessed upon acquiring a complete 5th dimensional orientation with reality – a total awareness that reality is experienced through the selection of postulates streaming into the individual's experience, beyond the control of any external force or outside influence.

Consciousness experienced under the individual's submission to outside forces demotes the individual to a 4th dimensional orientation with reality. An identity of the self persists, but conscious control of existence is restricted due to the perceptive mythology of being subject to an "outside world".

Eli Rook

Although the evolutionary leap into consciousness that occurred several thousand years ago was observably widespread, remnants of the pre-conscious mind persisted in the experience of nearly every conscious being on planet Earth. And due to its persistence, situations and circumstances perceived as being destructive toward conscious beings (and nature itself) manifest in various forms to this day.

Abominations such as crime, violence, and the violation of individual rights observed throughout history, and on through the beginning of the 21st century, all result from the disease of the mind - remnants of pre-conscious thought which entertain the illusion that a 4th dimensional orientation with reality is the defacto standard in which life experience must be conducted.

But today, standing in this new world looking back, we now clearly observe the bizarre, irrational events of ignorance, superstition, and violence occurring as a direct result of civilization's identity crisis – billions of conscious beings convinced that they were not God.

By personally reconciling that crisis of identity, you're poised to transition your life experience into a quantum trajectory where limiting remnants of the pre-conscious mind increasingly vanish amongst the individuals who conduct a life experience intersecting with your own.

The Big Fucking Secret

As your progress unfolds, the situations and circumstances you experience will be a far cry from what you perceived throughout the time you remained stuck in a fourth dimensional orientation with reality.

Now that you're able to consciously understand the fact that you are God, you suddenly occupy a vantage point from which you begin to reconcile the absurd irrationalities smeared upon civilization's chaotic past, vanishing their persistence as you advance.

You now clearly see how the irrational structures of authority littering the planet have persisted due to the will of semiconscious beings defaulting on their responsibility for self-guidance, self-leadership, and self-fulfillment.

You clearly see the irrational, dishonest, destructive actions, and limiting thoughts projected by conscious beings on planet Earth as nothing more than systemic results from the disease of the mind.

You yourself are guilty of programming the existence field to deliver unfavorable situations and circumstances into your life by allowing your fears to persist, by allowing yourself to be consumed by the valueless nonsense of others, and by defaulting to the archaic modality of living life convinced that you are not God.

But that chapter of your life is quickly coming to a close...

Eli Rook

With your quantum crossings into a 5th dimensional orientation with reality, you cure yourself of the consciousness disease, becoming less and less convinced that you are not God, in effect disintegrating the disease of the mind in others as you reorganize and shift the quantum triangulation they conduct into your life experience.

To obtain a wider perspective of how this disease of the mind played into the causality which persisted over the last several millenia, consider the most likely scenario in which human beings evolved into conscious beings.

Still not widely agreed upon, cutting edge research suggests the metaphysical confusion about conscious beings' role on planet Earth began when humankind suddenly leaped into consciousness en masse (circa 1000 B.C.)

Prior to the advent of consciousness, human beings were highly intelligent lifeforms, capable of complex mathematics, sophisticated architecture, and organized commerce, but did not enjoy the cognition of individuality and the control of existence we assume today.

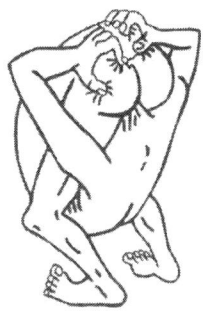

If you can imagine, it's proposed that only a few thousand years ago, the majority of human beings on planet Earth lived without consciousness, under the order of nature's automatic operating system.

The Big Fucking Secret

Then, for a variety of reasons including the pressure to survive as communication matured and civilization grew in complexity, humans one-by-one began to reorganize the way in which the mind was used, making individual shifts away from the automatic survival state of nature, into the dynamic creative state of consciousness.

As more human beings increasingly made the shift, more were soon to follow, until virtually all organized cultures suddenly leaped into consciousness in a hundredth-monkey-syndrome[5] type phenomenon.

The leap was unlike any phenomena observed in evolutionary biology, because it was not a biological change which occurred; *it was a conceptual change in orientation with reality.*

Since no scientific instrument or biological science can accurately measure perceptual changes in the mind, evidence of the leap into consciousness was uncovered through the study of linguistic expression observed in art and literature throughout history.

This is proposed under the premise that consciousness requires language, and consciousness is primarily harnessed through the use of metaphors, enabling a comprehensive understanding of one's own individual relationship to the existence field.

---

[5] The 100th Monkey Syndrome is a metaphorical expression of the phenomenon in which behavior and thought processes are acquired by lifeforms in absence of physical demonstration or explicit communication, also understood as "natural phenomena".

For instance, "I" is a metaphor expressing the self. The depth of meaning underlying such a metaphor cannot be harnessed by non-conscious beings, even highly intelligent lifeforms, such as primates.

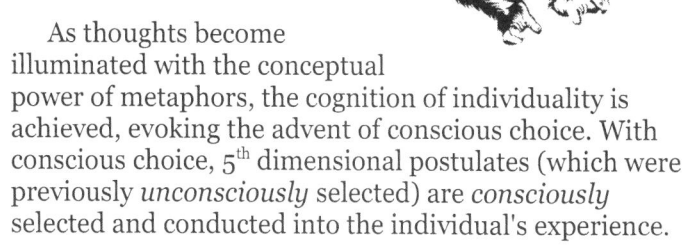

As thoughts become illuminated with the conceptual power of metaphors, the cognition of individuality is achieved, evoking the advent of conscious choice. With conscious choice, 5th dimensional postulates (which were previously *unconsciously* selected) are *consciously* selected and conducted into the individual's experience.

Through the rational management of conscious decisions, an individual achieves the capacity to manifest conditions for maximizing personal happiness and enriching the lives of others. This is accomplished in a manner that *far exceeds* the pace and efficacy produced by non-conscious lifeforms existing at the behest of nature.

WAKE UP!

With the advent of consciousness, the awareness of one's ability to manifest a specific desire is established, and with such awareness, the individual eventually "wake's up" to achieve the cognition that they control the entire realm existence they inhabit.

It's language that enables the outward expression of ideas and the inward introspection of the self, which are both prerequisites for the mind to be reorganized in a manner so it may harness consciousness.

The Big Fucking Secret

Consciousness is not a part of the brain. Consciousness itself has no single or specific physical location in the human body. Furthermore, there is no biological organ or part of the brain which guarantees consciousness[6].

Consciousness is also not an energy existing in the electromagnetic field that surrounds and permeates the body. Consciousness is *woven throughout existence*, and *harnessed* through an *organization of the mind*.

Before achieving the organization of the mind in which consciousness could be harnessed, human beings lived *without consciousness* under the command of nature's automatic operating system, under guidance in the form of auditory hallucinations in the right hemisphere of the brain.

Pre-conscious humans were ultimately "guided by voices" (not unlike what's experienced by schizophrenics, or those who experience religious-type trances today) and the automatic guidance pre-conscious human beings experienced wasn't unlike the automatic commands that other non-conscious lifeforms rely upon for survival.

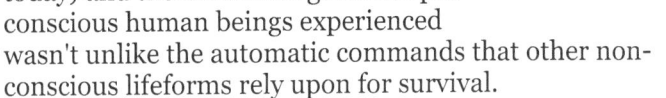

---

[6] Just because a human being possesses the biological requirements and information processing capacity necessary to harness consciousness, the *organization of the mind* required to harness consciousness is not guaranteed. Consciousness is a LEARNED phenomenon induced through the use of language. For instance, new born human beings achieve conscious stability only after the first few years of their life experience, and it's proposed that individuals throughout many indigenous tribal cultures had not achieved consciousness until several hundred years ago, far behind the mass leap experienced by cultures harnessing advanced language several millenia prior.

Eli Rook

The automatic guidance of nature is what drives birds to fly south for the winter, and salmon to swim back to the location whence they spawned. It orchestrates forest fires so pine cones can seed new trees and it drives tectonic shifts to reorganize geological surface conditions, facilitating renewed growth.

At the dawn of consciousness, *while still under the control of nature's automatic guidance system*, semiconscious human beings invented metaphorical gods as a means of expressing characteristics observed throughout nature, and as a utility for the justification of an individual's actions.

For instance, thunder was explained as being performed by the God of Thunder and rain was explained as being a miracle of the Rain Gods. The decision to plunder a village was exercised as a charge of divine purpose.

Imagined gods were given credibility for everything witnessed in nature, as well as the social interactions amongst non-conscious beings (e.g. gods and goddesses of love, war, fertility, laughter, etc.)

Then, as the sophistication of language advanced the ability for human beings to harness greater intelligence, the voices of imagined gods increasingly conflicted, ripening the conditions in which the leap into consciousness could be induced.

The Big Fucking Secret

During the breakdown of the pre-conscious mind, a string of movements to consolidate the many external gods into a single almighty external God[7] persisted until a consolidation was largely adopted, sometime before the Golden Age of Greece.

As a leap into consciousness marked the departure from a pre-conscious past of multiple imagined gods, a comprehensive understanding of what consciousness truly delivered into the lives of human beings was only garnered by a few, and the mystical illusion of an almighty God ("Exo-God") bore acceptance in the minds of lower class peasants and slaves.

Aside from those enlightened few who reached a fifth dimensional conscious orientation with reality *(whom we'll refer to as The Illuminati)* a habitual gravitation toward the automatic guidance of the pre-conscious mind persisted, paralyzing the majority of human populations in a state of limited consciousness.

Although the majority of individuals who made the leap into consciousness achieved an identity of the self, and enjoyed the ability to exercise conscious thought, they still had not yet achieved the full awareness of their relationship with the existence field.

Thus, a mythology that external forces and outside influences controlled existence *(which contradicts to the essence of consciousness)* dishonestly plagued the minds of conscious beings.

---

[7] Historically observed in acts such as Abraham smashing his father's idols, and Akhenaten's attempt to bring an end to Egyptian polytheism.

This made way for the manifestation of unfavorable situations and circumstances to befall those who remained entrenched in a fourth dimensional orientation with reality, and with the disease of the mind causing conscious beings to seek external guidance, a ruling class of individuals, *who were clearly aware of the fact that they were God*, assumed rule over the semiconscious masses.

Any individual who failed to conceptualize how God is *a controlling utility woven throughout The All* continued to seek automatic guidance from other conscious beings who assumed "authority" as the administrators of Exo-God's will.

Outside the ruling elite class of church elders, imperialist thugs, and civic manipulators, the vast majority of civilization remained suspended in a semiconscious state for over two millennia, socially engineered to live as domesticated peasants, voluntarily suppressed through their own choice to accept irrational beliefs derived from Exo-God mythology, and promoted through destructive collectivist "higher causes".

The disease of irrational beliefs littering the existence field around planet Earth mutated into guilt-fostering religions, force-backed governments, and value-draining philosophies, which were supported by individuals ignorant about the inherent cosmic power available to all conscious beings.

The Big Fucking Secret

As civilization pressed onward after the dark ages, increased intelligence through the mass circulation of books sparked The Renaissance. Then, geographic exploration and global commerce further diminished the ruling elite's economic and mental domineering of the peasant class.

Monarchical empires began to crumble, and savvy businessmen largely assumed rule over semiconscious beings, orchestrating the modern socialistic slavery systems employed across the developed world today.

As a result of the business plan executed by the modern ruling faction, led by international captains of industry, myths of Exo-God have become increasingly laughable amongst the intelligent majority of civilization during the last two hundred years.

And today, a barrage of factors are increasingly soaring to liberate record numbers of individuals from the old world once and for all.

The educational infrastructure and social utilities established on the world wide web aim to liberate the ignorant.

The technological advancements poised to support the basic needs of human life aim to liberate the resource-deprived.

The economic conditions we face aim to catapult civilization into an abundant new era of open commerce as fiat currencies are systematically obliterated.

Eli Rook

The end result, in tune with countless other factors at play right now, is a mass awaking of conscious beings all around planet earth, enduring a perpetual series of quantum crossings into 5th dimensional orientation with reality.

Just as early conscious beings vanished the Greek and Roman gods while at the brink of a new conscious awareness, conscious beings today vanish the myths of Exo-God and irrational structures of authority while advancing toward illuminated 5th dimensional conscious orientation.

Just as historic Illuminati were instrumental in ushering in the explosion of knowledge during the Golden Age of Greece, liberating the serfs of the medieval age, and toppling monarchial empires around the globe during The Enlightenment, the modern Illuminati[8] now advance humanity to new levels of social, intellectual, and economic liberation through the calculated demolition of the political ruling class.

The human race is speeding into its final ascent toward a new world of sovereignty, prosperity, immortality, and abundance.

The manifestation of this ascent is cleverly obscured in the chaos as it's perpetually transmuted into order...

problem?

---

[8] While those who control global industry are deemed evil for social, political, and environmental influence, all forward movement produced by their efforts leads to a single, ultimately valiant end result: the final collapse of politics, religion, and even philosophy – and conditions for a non-coercive sovereign new world of prosperity and safety to render.

The Big Fucking Secret
You're observing the paradigm-shift unfolding all around you...

It's observed in the rise of alternative currencies outcompeting fiat currencies, enabling the honest utility of money to deliver growing value in the life experience of all conscious beings.

It's observed in the adoption of sovereign, libertarian based structures for civic organization that outcompete force-backed government regulatory schemes, which enable lazy dishonest parasites to extract unearned power and wealth from the populace.

It's being celebrated as innovative geniuses spearhead the mass availability of technological resources, providing free energy for water purification, food cultivation, transportation, and communication – outcompeting stagnated government-entrenched corporate hoaxes.

Again, these manifestations ultimately transpire not as a result of any event occurring beyond your control!

As you establish a new array of fifth dimensional postulates and you render these postulates into your experience (which we'll be discussing in later chapters), you'll ascend to the power-position of a modern Illuminati, manifesting – in real-time – the new world you desire to inhabit.

Eli Rook

The new world you wish to live in will not manifest because a specific organization or group came forward to "save you"... It will render in your experience due to your persistent effort to maintain a 5th dimensional orientation with reality, in turn illuminating every conscious being on planet Earth, changing the quantum position from which they conduct their existence into your life experience.

And as you conduct yourself in this manner, the change occurring all around you will absolutely blow your mind!

When conscious beings choose to reject the mythology that outside influences rule over them, when no external force is blamed or credited for an individual's experience in the existence field, what kind of conditions do you suspect will transpire on planet Earth?

Imagine millions of conscious individuals, with the light of God in their eyes, intentionally pursuing the lives they were meant to live – free of guilt, fear, irrationality, and submission to higher authorities of religions and governments... Liberated from the manipulations of irrational philosophical constructs?

Imagine the mass cleansing of chaotic frequencies from a civilization separated from its identity over several millenia... Imagine events transpiring all around the planet as order increasingly springs forth out of chaos, like a phoenix rising...

The Big Fucking Secret

The source of this massive shift lies in your OWN PERSONAL STANCE to take full responsibility for your experience in the existence field... Your explosive decision to command forth the life experience you desire!

Let's explore the underlying conditions you must establish in order to accomplish such a feat.

Eli Rook

The Big Fucking Secret

CHAPTER 6

Clear your desktop.

Dump the trash. REBOOT.

You are God.

You control existence.

You'll consciously use the mind, brain, and body to emit a pulsation of energy that programs the existence field to move you in a trajectory toward desired events *which already exist* in the fifth dimension.

As those fifth dimensional postulates "render" in your life experience, and you gather confidence in your control over the existence field, you'll organize your efforts towards manifesting *complete self-fulfillment*.

The following chapters introduce:
THE SELF-FULFILLMENT FORMULA

Upon consciously utilizing the Self-Fulfillment Formula to encounter favorable, noticeable results, you'll explode with enthusiasm, enthralled by the cognition of your endless navigable future, and continue transitioning into a complete 5th dimensional orientation with reality – becoming an active resident in the Civilization of Luminiferous Ascension.

The Self-Fulfillment Formula is certainly nothing new... It's been expressed, expanded upon, deconstructed, and reassembled by countless authors, but its implementation has remained curiously elusive...

The Big Fucking Secret

The Big Fucking Secret aims to rectify that issue once and for all.

Before reading this book, you may have come across other books discussing manifestation and "creation", and even more books discussing consciousness, magik, the occult, and a slew of other topics...

A large number of people have read those books, and while much of the information was codified and proven, a very small number of people actually get REAL LIFE RESULTS from what they read.

So what's the big difference in The Big Fucking Secret?

What's the magic ingredient that enables the reader to break through into cosmic-level cognitions in such a short time, which such little content to review?

So far, there's no mention of positive thinking or habits of highly successful people, mystical rituals, spiritual principles, self-help cliches, or the Law of Attraction techniques...

Yet why is this book so powerful?

Why does it deliver such an impact?

Why is it so well received by its readers?

Perhaps because it brings you closer to understanding why you're here, and exactly what's going on in the multidimensional matrix of existence...

Perhaps because it offers the <u>raw honesty</u> that your brain is a cosmic quantum-computer controlling every last particle in existence (and you spent the majority of your life being convinced otherwise!!)

Very few other spirit-science or self-development books happen to fully communicate the one thing *you must know* in order to use <u>ALL</u> the power you can harness:

<u>YOU</u> ARE GOD.

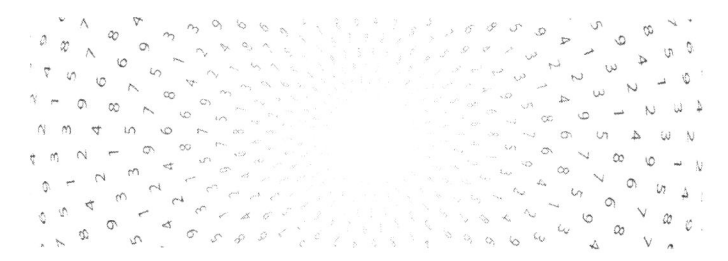

<u>YOU</u> CONTROL EXISTENCE.

By understanding what you've read so far about the evolution of consciousness in human beings on planet Earth, and how the mind, brain, and body works in multidimensional unison with the existence field, you hold a wider view of how the manifestation of the *old world* resulted from the consciousness disease (and the simple cure that vanishes humanity's sordid past.)

In the process of obtaining a wider-scope view, your quantum crossings from a 4th dimensional orientation with reality into a 5th dimensional orientation have been induced; enabling you to further render the Civilization of Luminiferous Ascension here on planet Earth...

These quantum crossings will persist as you continue to deepen the cognition that you are God and you control existence.

The Big Fucking Secret

The ageless "Self-Fulfillment Formula" is what you've been *unconsciously* using your entire life to manifest the favorable situations and circumstances you've encountered... And you might have continued using it unconsciously had you not read The Big Fucking Secret!

You'll now learn how to use this Formula CONSCIOUSLY, guiding a stream of emotional, psychological, and material fulfillment into your life.

You'll consciously harness multidimensional power using the technology of the mind, brain, and body to emit a pulsation of energy into The All, transitioning your quantum triangulation toward that of your fifth dimensional postulates *which are destined*.

Upon mastering your ability to consciously use The Self-Fulfillment Formula, *and enjoying the soaring confidence you achieve*, you'll increasingly gain awareness of the cosmic symphony you've been conducting since your birth, and vanish the persistence of any lingering unfavorable element from your past.

The ill feelings associated with the pathological thoughts you established throughout your life experience will all but disappear. Their supporting neural pathways and cellular-level information will essentially become dormant, virtually immune to restimulation.

The events of your past will have little bearing on your future as you gain complete control of your consciousness experience.

Eli Rook
An exciting new world is astir!

The speed in which you solidify your new world triangulation will vary based on the integrated health of your mind and body. So let's do a little housekeeping...

Your level of health is inextricably linked to the degree in which you consciously control existence.

Your DNA, the basis upon which your physical form persists, was biologically passed on to you directly from your parents.

While the genetic code in your DNA determined your initial physiology, your thoughts have continuously altered your DNA, and governed your ability to consciously control the evolvement of your physical form.

Your thoughts are also the ultimate determining factor in the situations and circumstances you manifest, so with regard to external forces, your thoughts exist at the root of every physiological condition you endured, since you became conscious. (This includes the onset of environmental toxicity, viruses, and other potential old world perils[9].)

---

[9] Your thoughts are ultimately responsible for your body's alkalinity, which if properly maintained, provides conditions for a physiological environment where disease and illness cannot exist.

The Big Fucking Secret

Due to the circumstances surrounding your entry point into the current biological state of human evolution, your body still requires adequate hydration, breathing, and nutrition from food sources.

And due to the circumstances surrounding your acquisition of the disease of the mind, your ability to thrive physiologically has been impeded by environmental toxins in the water your drink, the food you eat, the air your breathe, as well as the radiation you absorb[10].

Toxins accumulated in your cells, and radiation absorbed in the electromagnetic field surrounding and permeating your body hinders cellular communication, and therefore cellular replication, which is necessary for a thriving physiology.

While you could technically cleanse your cells of these toxins exclusively with your thoughts, along with extensive fasting – herbal and homeopathic regimens, or therapeutic procedures may expedite the process.

Cleansing formulas and therapies are widely available, and vary in efficacy based on the quality and combination of ingredients, and the unique characteristics of an individual's physiology.

---

[10] Your thoughts are ultimately responsible for rendering the world around you, therefore it was you who guided your consciousness experience into an increasingly toxic version of planet Earth.

Eli Rook

Healing one's electromagnetic field could technically be achieved through the application of healthy conscious thoughts as well, but various technologies are available to expedite that process.

(The only way to shield your body from ongoing cellular toxicity in the old world is to avoid ingesting toxic food and breathing impure air.)

In addition to breathing, hydration, cleansing, nutrition, and electromagnetic repair, optimum health is achieved through engaging in physical activity (primarily raising your arrested heartbeat daily for 30 minutes), as well as engaging in a sufficient amount of sleep (4-8 hours nightly).

The mind and body are a single integrated unit.

Thus, maintaining high levels of cellular communication and cellular replication in the body – as well as a properly harmonized electromagnetic field – yields a biological state in which the energetic resources of the brain are no longer unnecessarily drained, enabling the mind to be fully utilized toward its optimum capacity.

With the brain free of its unnecessary requirements for managing an overstressed cellular system, the capacity for integrated thinking improves, senses are heightened, and the cognition of one's control over existence is better sustained.

Yet the mind and brain can only operate together in their most optimum capacity through rational, honest integrated thinking.

The Big Fucking Secret

In hindsight, your existing neurology and cellular-level memory storage is now plagued with the irrationalities of your old world past, which brings us to the crux of our departure into the subject of health.

Your thoughts are at the epicenter of your health.

Your pulsation of energy is a combination of your thoughts and your DNA vibration.

While your DNA's vibration can be slightly altered over time, your thoughts can be immediately altered.

And because your thoughts change your DNA's vibration, effectively improving your health at the most fundamental level, thoughts will be at the forefront of our focus throughout The Big Fucking Secret.

Your brain has close to 100 billion brain cells, called neurons, many of which connect through an estimated 100 trillion neural pathways.

Energy constantly flows through your neural network, in the form of beta, alpha, theta, delta, beta2, and gamma brainwaves.

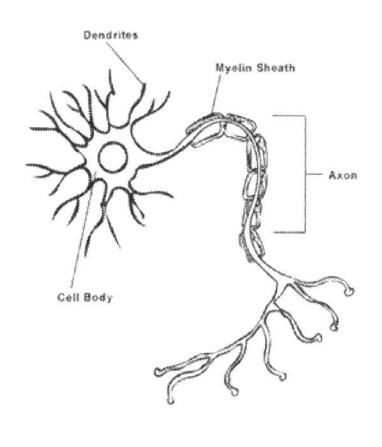

Your entire being is in a specific brainwave state at any one time, and the brain enters specific brainwave states to best utilize its information processing capabilities.

Eli Rook

Beta is an information gathering brainwave state. Beta brainwaves emanate from the dendrites which extend from the neural cell body. Dendrites constantly receive information and pass it on to the cell body of the neuron.

β

Alpha is an information processing brainwave state. Alpha brainwaves emanate from the cell body of the neuron as information collected by the dendrites is passed toward the cell nucleus.

α

Theta is an information storage brainwave state. Theta brainwaves emanate from the cellular nucleus of the neuron. As information collected by the dendrite is successful processed through the cell body, it's stored in the nucleus.

Θ

Delta is an information transmitting brainwave state. Delta brainwaves emanate from the axon, which extends from the cell body, carrying the impulse directive of the neuron.

Δ

Beta2 is an information integration brainwave state. Beta2 brainwaves emanate from the synaptic terminals extending from the axon, which emit a variety of neurotransmitters, and connect to other neurons, dendrites, and synaptic terminals.

β

Gamma is an information management brainwave state. Emanating from entire neural circuits, Gamma brainwaves dynamically optimize the regulation of all the other brainwaves, promoting electromagnetic harmony in a particular circuit; so the overall energetic pulsation of information may persist in a free-flowing, high-frequency capacity.

Γ

The Big Fucking Secret

Understand that the mind gravitates toward thoughts drawn forth from the information within the neural circuits holding the strongest electromagnetic currents.

Thus a varying degree of polarization in the electromagnetic makeup of a thought carries ramifications effecting how an individual feels, and the natural direction in which contiguous thoughts flow.

When a Gamma brainwave state is induced, energy flowing through a particular circuit is neutralized to a degree, and the energetic resources of the brain are most optimally utilized, allowing the mind accesses a range of information from the brain which serves the individual's most favorable self-interest.

With the harmony of electromagnetic polarization in the neural circuits, the conditions for consciousness to best be utilized to reinforce and expand the health of one's brain and body may be obtained.

So henceforth, our focus will be upon exploring the mode in which Gamma brainwaves serve the dynamics of the brain to harness the power requirements for your ascension into a 5th dimensional orientation with reality.

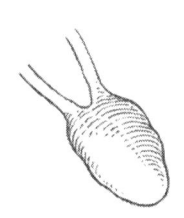

This version of The Big Fucking Secret will skip a comprehensive assessment of the functionality in each region in the brain, and instead focus only on the hypothalamus, existing just above the brainstem, and the pineal gland adjacent to the cerebellum.

Eli Rook

<u>The hypothalamus</u> is chemical factory, largely responsible for the activities of the autonomic nervous system, and the production of neuropeptides and neurohormones that guide the body in experiencing certain physical sensations as emotions persist.

<u>The pineal gland</u> is a biomagnetic receptor receiving "etheric" information encoded throughout the existence field[11], and produces DMT, a neurotransmitter carrying the pineal gland's directives to the neural network.

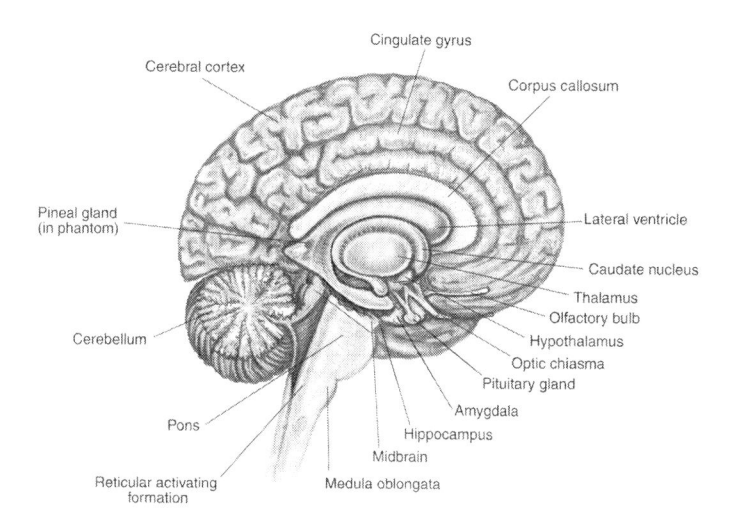

A 4th dimensional orientation with reality is typically sustained as the conscious being allows the hypothalamus to serve the brain and body's functionality. But upon achieving enough Gamma energy, conditions are established in the brain so the pineal gland may take over.

---

[11] Yet still not fully known, "etheric" data is presumably gravity-coded.

The Big Fucking Secret

When the mind accesses information processed in the brain under the directive of the pineal gland, the mind may organize that information as thought which promotes the ascension into a 5th dimensional orientation with reality.

With the human organism functioning in it's most optimum capacity, both physiologically, psychologically, and energetically, a host of abilities naturally come forth.

Depending on the unique constraints of an individual's DNA, skills such as clairvoyance, advanced healing abilities, and a host of other "supernatural" powers are intensified. And with the advent of consciousness, the human organism can guide the use of these abilities in ways which may *enhance* or *diminish* the quality of their life experience, and the quality of intersecting life experiences conducted by other conscious beings.

CIVILIZATION OF THE UNIVERSE	CIVILIZATION ON EARTH
HEALTH, WEALTH, SAFETY, AND FUN	CHALLENGE ACCEPTED

So herein lies the challenge you will overcome using The Self-Fulfillment Formula and all the knowledge presented in The Big Fucking Secret...

Through the function of the pineal gland, your brain has the capacity to receive all the information (frequency, vibration, etc.) existing throughout the entire multidimensional existence field.

Yet the brain has an overall processing capacity stifled by an inherent biological limitation[12]. So even at its optimum processing capacity, the range of information processed at any one time is only a fraction of all the information in the existence field.

Furthermore, due to the fact that your conscious mind processes information at a fraction of the speed achieved by your brain, you draw forth an even smaller range of information from the existence field in your conscious thoughts.

Plus, the brain's capability to serve the conscious mind may be degraded due to channeling of resources necessary in addressing the aberrations of low cellular communication and electromagnetic disharmony.

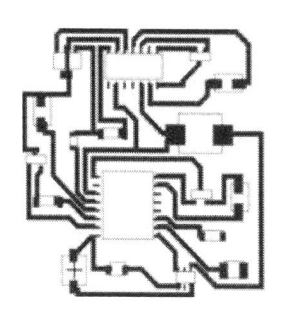

But perhaps the most significant challenge you face in fully utilizing the mind and brain to induce lasting quantum crossings into a 5th dimensional orientation with reality is the corruption of data *in your existing neural circuitry*.

---

[12] While the physical brain has a limited information processing capacity, the mind's ability to integrate information is ultimately limitless. The processing limitations in the brain will eventually be overcome as we reach The Singularity.

The Big Fucking Secret

Throughout your life you've been building intricate neural pathways, which support all the data you've acquired, and all the knowledge you've integrated.

The harmonization of energy conducted in the circuits of connecting neural pathways is determined by the degree of accuracy in which you've integrated all the knowledge you possess with *eternal multidimensional honesty*.

When you possess knowledge which is not correctly integrated – *meaning you have drawn conclusions about existence which are not compatible with existence* - you hold mythological conclusions as undeniable "truths".

PIE in the SKY

Because mythological thoughts do not harmonize with The All, energy flowing through the supporting neural circuitry is compromised in effect, vibrating in a unpolarized fashion, resulting in an electromagnetic imbalance within various elements of the circuit.

Overtime, if the offset polarity in the neural circuitry is not neutralized, the actual health of the neurons diminish, and their ability to conduct energy becomes dysfunctional...

Eventually, they may even burn out!

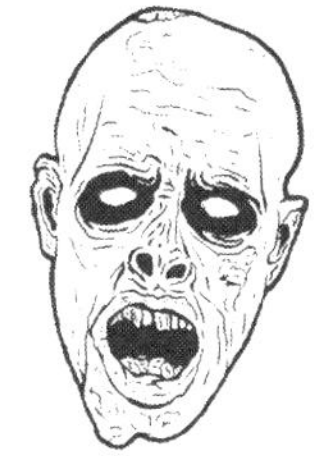

Eli Rook

Deeply entrenched mythological thoughts also hinder the brain's ability to properly cycle through the various brainwaves, potentially sequestering an individual in a zombie-like Beta brainwave *loop* – paralyzing the subject in a perceptive trance; rarely obtaining or integrating the data necessary to support their psychological growth, and ability to experience personal happiness.

All consciously established offset polarity stems from the disease of the mind, and its persistence throughout the neural makeup *promotes* an ongoing irrational conceptualization of reality.

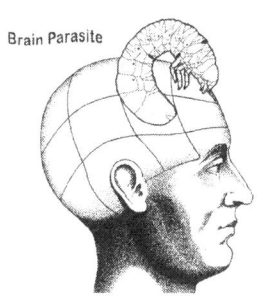

One could go as far as categorizing the irrational thoughts infecting the neurology as *parasitic*, due to their ability to promote neural functionality that influences any new data entering the system – *compromising the data* - and further denigrating the individual's ability to accurately conceptualize reality.

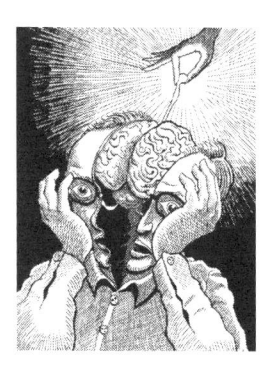

In this modality, the pineal gland is relegated to become a dormant gateway to the cosmos, and situations and circumstances culminate to support an overwhelming "truth" that the world is ending, life is ultimately meaningless, and we all die and go to heaven anyways...

"So why care!?"

The Big Fucking Secret

When afflicted with disease of the mind, mysticism, or "being convinced that you are not God", a human being will conduct thought in a manner that allows the parasitic influence of the neural circuitry to enter their Pulsation, manifesting a waking existence in which the disease of the mind goes <u>unnoticed</u>!

The erroneous "truth" that you are not God is programmed into your neurology, which factors into your Pulsation, which manifests a tangible world around you, full of events, facts, and PROOF supporting the erroneous "TRUTH" that <u>you are not God</u>!!

The onset of this disease occurs from two elements which all human beings face in their childhood, usually beginning around the age of 7.

<u>Not being teachable</u> – When you are not open to receive information you encounter, dendrites fail to pass the information they receive into the cell body of the neuron. (This is actually a result of an Alpha conflict in cell body.)

<u>Not integrating data</u> – Even after the information is captured by the dendrites in Beta, passed through the cell body in Alpha, and absorbed into the neuron in Theta, if the information is not transmitted to other neurons through Delta and Beta2, there will be no healthy integration of data, and a potentially imbalanced Theta or Delta charge can mount.

Eli Rook

As a growing child experiencing the most favorable circumstances and situations, you were either closed off to the information presented about the fact that you are God, or you received the data, but didn't integrate it.

In cases where less favorable circumstances transpired, you may have encountered irrational dogmas about the mythical Exo-God, or dishonest philosophical constructs about ethics and morals, during which you failed to reject the information because you didn't have the integrated knowledge required to conclude that you were being exposed to harmful mythology!

In any case, the elusive parasitic mythology that you are not God – vibrating in your neurology – is constantly contributing to the pulsation of energy you emit. And if you continue to walk the Earth, being convinced that you are not God, you'll remain stuck in a 4th dimensional orientation with reality – voluntarily seeking a date with Death.

But fortunately, you've been able to successfully reprogram your neurology to a degree, rejecting some of the mythologies you've encountered, and because of that, you can engage in quantum crossings into a 5th dimensional orientation with reality =)

The Big Fucking Secret

Your manifestation of The Big Fucking Secret is a subtle demonstration of the power you wield in this regard, and it's just a blip on the radar when you look at the VAST opportunity you face with this wider view of existence!

You face virtually *no limitations* to the expansion of your psychological growth, and the command you hold over your health; as well as your ability to ascend into a complete 5th dimensional orientation with reality!

Even the constraints in your DNA are no longer a limitation, as you have the ability to fully activate your DNA over time, no matter what "disadvantaged" conditions you biologically inherited!!

With your conscious thoughts, you can reprogram your neural circuitry and harmonize your brainwave functionality; emitting a pulsation of energy that yields more favorable situations and circumstances; bringing you closer to the manifestation of all your destined 5th dimensional postulates!!!

Various therapies, devices, and technologies exist, designed to eliminate your habitual maintenance of the parasitic neural pathways you've established, and repair the corrupted information stored in your cellular makeup (which has been denigrating your DNA's vibration). But the authors of this book propose the only real viable solution, which is an ever-present, guaranteed, no-cost, non-mystical remedy for the condition you've established in your head:

Eli Rook

"Think about what you're thinking about, and change what you think about, so it's congruent with who you are meant to be."

Imagine a neural pathway as the road that energy travels down each time you think a certain thought.

The more you think a particular thought, the more energy flows through the pathway. The energy flow gives the pathway precedence, causing the thought associated with that pathway to become an evermore apparent "truth".

You cannot eliminate that neural pathway, but over time – *as you cease to engage in a particular thought process* – its parasitic nature diminishes. The old neural pathways eventually cease operating to your detriment. The magnetic pull of that pathway declines, and it eventually becomes all but dormant.

By being aware of your thoughts and constantly directing your thoughts toward strengthening the neural pathways that serve your benefit brings the neurology into greater harmony – causing your Pulsation to program the multidimensional matrix for increasing favorability – so your destined 5th dimensional postulates begin to render *in the most optimum timeframe possible.*

The Big Fucking Secret

To move forward, a commitment to being teachable, and learning new information is the bridge to your new home in the Civilization of Luminiferous Ascension.

A commitment to thinking and integrating information honestly is the vehicle by which you will travel upon that bridge.

And your mental and physical effort to apply information as a contribution to the cosmic reservoir of happiness and creativity govern the speed in which you *permanently* cross that bridge.

The Self-Fulfillment Formula further introduced in the next chapter will illustrate some basic directives for accomplishing this...

But before we can utilize The Self-Fulfillment formula we must expand the knowledge we covered about the thinking process with a rundown of your emotional intelligence, in order to assemble a more integrated conceptualization of the human experience.

Eli Rook

The Big Fucking Secret

CHAPTER 7

The primary reason you exist is actually quite simple...

"Why you are here" is no longer a mystery...

The primary reason you exist is to EXPERIENCE PERSONAL HAPPINESS!

That's it! That's why you're here!

You exist for nothing more than to experience happiness.

And beyond the primary importance of your own personal happiness exists a second objective: to *serve others*, and help *them* experience happiness.

Personal happiness is intrinsic to the nature of conscious life... It's why you live... It's the ultimate responsibility of being a conscious being.

But when you live in contradiction to your nature – when you fail to meet your ultimate responsibility – you experience degraded levels of personal happiness...

So it behooves you to live your life in harmony with your nature as a conscious being, to control existence in your favor, as you're destined to.

The symmetry you hold on the path to become who-you-are-meant-to-be is solely governed by the thoughts you maintain. And your personal happiness is achieved, or evaded, to the degree in which you hold symmetry.

The Big Fucking Secret

Happiness is both consciously experienced in the mind as thoughts and emotions, and physically experienced in the body as a variety of feelings.

All emotion, and all the feelings through which they're expressed, are all derived from your conscious and unconscious thoughts.

Existence is comprised of mass, energy, gravity, and consciousness, and there exist electromagnetic fields which surround, permeate, and interconnect amongst all forms of physical matter.

So to better serve your ongoing quantum crossings, we will refer to the electromagnetic life-force energy of each living thing as mind.

We'll loosely use the term as it's applied to life-force fields which emanate from flora and fungi... More aptly as it's applied to life-force fields emanating from fauna... And *precisely* as it's applied to the electromagnetic fields that surround and permeate the bodies of conscious human beings.

Flora for Fauna

Referring to the mind in these various designations, we'll also clarify that the ability of flora to interact with its environment is inherent to its cellular level intelligence.

Similarly, we'll specify that the environmental interaction of fauna is also inherent to its cellular level intelligence, but set apart from flora with a distinction that the central processing directive is provided by a brain.

Eli Rook

We will also playfully – and metaphorically – refer to the electromagnetic force emanating from inorganic materials as *mind*, simply to fulfill the objective of demonstrating the phenomenon of how consciousness interacts with the entire existence field, on a quantum physical level.

With those parameters outlined, we'll establish that it's through the mind that living organisms interact with both organic and inorganic matter found throughout nature, including all that's constructed by conscious beings (outside of nature).

The human organism has evolved in biological complexity to an extent that its brain is capable of facilitating the mind's ability to harness consciousness, thus uniquely setting it apart from every non-conscious life form.

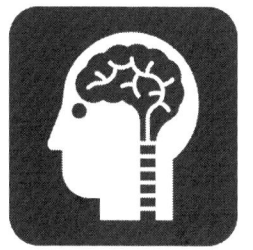

While other highly intelligent, Earth-evolved life forms endure limited processing power in their brains, and face conceptual challenges within the limits of their intelligence, human beings evolved in biological complexity to acquire the processing power necessary for the development of language, enabling conceptual challenges faced in the pre-conscious era to be overcome; so a new organization of the mind could be achieved to harness consciousness.

The Big Fucking Secret

With specific regard to all other fauna, the mind receives instructions from nature's automatic operating system, programming the neurology of the brain accordingly.

Conversely, a human being programs the neurology of its brain in a similar manner, but with a distinction...

Through the ability to harness consciousness, a human individual gains *the* *capacity* to administer control over how the brain operates, thus dually engaging in nature's automatic operating system AND the self-guided operating system of consciousness.

Just like any other organism endowed with a brain, conscious beings use logic and reason to go about surviving. Yet the mind of a conscious being has the unique capacity to perform *conscious* decisions, making choices to think and act in ways which may contradict the automatic guidance of nature, and the guidance of other conscious beings.

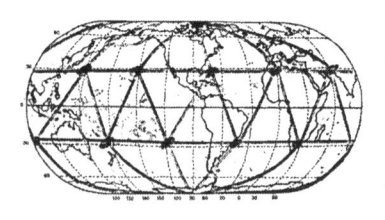

To illustrate the seeming *dichotomy* in which all life exists apart from conscious beings, consider the "world" of consciousness as being a world *layered upon* the "world" of nature.

And to illustrate the *connectedness* of nature with consciousness, consider the world of consciousness *permeating* the world of nature.

With the disease of the mind, a conscious being no longer exists in the world of consciousness, permeating nature to serve the purpose of conscious existence...

Under the disease of the mind, the conscious being experiences the *illusion* of being subject to nature, ultimately conceiving the "world" of consciousness as Exo-God.

The non-conscious mind of all living things operates through a default 4th dimensional orientation with reality – the mind of nature.

But the conscious mind operates through a default 5th dimensional orientation with reality – the mind of God – and experiences a 4th dimensional orientation with reality upon acquiring the consciousness disease (being convinced that you are not God).

So with the utility of consciousness, how does one find <u>direction</u> toward curing the disease of the mind?

Thoughts, emotions, sensory interpretation, and physiological feelings makeup the cognitive experience of all mammalian life, yet human beings are set apart through their ability to experience all of these elements through *conscious introspection*.

All that is experienced in life can be consciously conceived, expressed, pulled apart and put back together, shared and reenacted, metaphorically transmuted, and re-experienced in the mind.

Oh! What an endless array of magical worlds hum within the minds of conscious beings!

The Big Fucking Secret

The brain is responsible for sequencing emotions which reflect conscious and unconscious thoughts, and evoke physiological reactions in the body, called feelings.

Feelings always reflect a degree of <u>favorability</u>, subject to the unique conscious interpretation of the individual. The favorability scale of any feeling generally tips to one side: either feeling good, or feeling bad.

Feelings are ultimately a substrate of the emotional and cognitive experience in the mind.

A unique distinction in regards to feelings further illustrates the dynamism of consciousness...

Non-conscious organisms merely encounter the physiological sensation of feelings under the directive of the brain (guided by nature's automatic operating system) and physically <u>react</u> accordingly.

Conscious beings also encounter the physiological sensation of feelings under the directive of the brain, yet the conscious individual is unique in that it may <u>respond</u> consciously to alter the way it feels. This can be performed without regard to stimuli from external forces or outside influences, again setting the conscious being apart from all non-conscious life forms, and demonstrating the conscious individual's innate control over its individual life experience.

While feelings may initially transpire beyond an individual's control, feelings can be consciously utilized to obtain *guidance,* first interpreting the information processed by the brain (which caused the feeling) and then responding with a thought to guide the conscious experience into a variant feeling (if desired).

By responding in a favorable manner, a healthy contribution to the brain's ongoing neural programming is achieved, and the speed in which any destined 5th dimensional postulates are being rendered potentially increases.

Guidance is obtained through the accurate interpretation of emotion.

The thoughts and emotions experienced in the mind, simultaneously processed in the brain, are inextricably linked to the feelings which are physiologically experienced in the body.

Yet the emotional component of a thought is largely automatic, and often experienced as a physiological feeling *in advance* of your ability to gather an interpretive cognition about the emotional component of the thought.

Because a thought lies at the root of every feeling, and feelings are experienced in advance of your cognitive insight, emotions seem to exist *just beyond* your control.

Yet, you still have the capacity to introspectively draw forth a conceptualization about the emotion which is expressed through the physiological feeling, and then consciously choose how to respond in order to control existence in your favor.

You're in continuous control of the *response* elicited in the face of ANY emotion... And herein lies a significant opportunity for operational error, which may contribute to the persistence of the consciousness disease.

The Big Fucking Secret

The speed of information processing in the conscious mind is significantly less than the speed of information processing in the brain. Therefore, the brain processes more information that you can consciously access in real-time.

Because the mind, brain, and body are a single integrated unit, the feelings you experience in the body are integrally connected to the information processed by the brain, and the "feedback" you consciously obtain from the physiological onset of an emotion can be used to access information from the brain which is not consciously apparent.

The feedback process is referred to as the *emotional guidance system* because the information gathered is used to direct thought into new integrations of knowledge, which ultimately guide the outcome of a conscious decision.

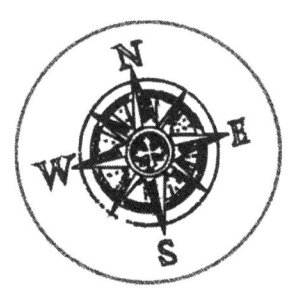

Your rational and objective interpretation of the feelings you encounter while using the emotional guidance system can accelerate your ability to achieve personal happiness.

But when feelings are not rationally interpreted, and not responded upon in a manner which best suits the manifestation of one's desires, inherently dishonest thoughts serve imbalanced electromagnetic frequencies that infect the neurology.

Eli Rook

With specific regard to using the emotional guidance system in navigating toward the quantum triangulation of a 5th dimensional postulate, imbalanced frequencies in the neurology generate "resistance", and could be understood as "counter-intention", infecting the pulsation of energy one emits into The All.

If resistant thoughts support a parasitically infected neural circuit, the unfavorable feeling in the body will persist, or increase with intensity.

But if the meaning derived from the conceptualization of an emotional state is consciously steered into a wide-scope rational integration of knowledge, established to serve the increased symmetry of your Pulsation, you will be acting in accordance with your nature as a conscious being, and eventually experience happiness – fulfilling your purpose for living.

The feelings experienced through most emotions generally have a specific level of favorability with little variation, while other feelings can be experienced with widely varying levels of favorability.

For instance, the emotion of anger, which would normally be described as feeling bad, and reflect an unfavorable condition experienced in the brain, could be consciously interpreted as a good feeling, due to its utility in that specific moment. The "bad" feeling of anger could be used to muster the will power to take an important action, initiate self-defense, or focus on a solution with greater intensity. In such a case, the favorability of anger is extremely high, and in some cases *necessary* for survival.

The Big Fucking Secret

The favorability of any emotion that's encountered is ultimately a subjective cognition, and can only be judged by the individual experiencing the emotion. Therefore you, and only you, can understand how to read your own emotional guidance system.

The techniques and methods in which you read its guidance are ultimately obtained through your own awareness, effort, and discovery, but we will briefly cover its basic yes/no/maybe operation to establish a foundation for practice.

How To Get Multidimensional Answers From The Brain

You are a multidimensional conscious being emitting a pulsation of energy which is determined by the sum of your conscious and unconscious thoughts, and the vibration of your DNA.

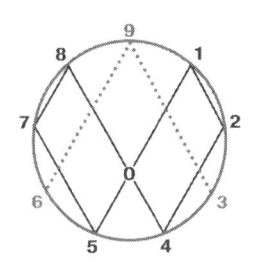

The quantum triangulation of your waking experience is in constant flux, and you either *are* – or *are not* – transitioning along a trajectory *symmetrical* with the-life-you-are-meant-live, which is a series of destined 5th dimensional postulates.

All the 5th dimensional postulates which adhere to your current trajectory render in your life experience based on the laws of physics as time passes by.

Your brain manages to know exactly where you are, and where you need to go next, with laser precision.

It also delivers a physiological state in the body which reflects the integration of all its data.

Eli Rook

Because the brain is a multidimensional processor of information, you can derive a yes/no/maybe response to almost any question you ask it – past, present, or future.

But do note, if the health of your cellular makeup is less than optimum, if the neural pathways in your brain carry parasitic electromagnetic charges, and if the breadth of your integrated knowledge is limited, or inaccurate, your ability to correctly interpret the guidance you receive will be hindered to a degree.

Therefore constantly engaging in a healthy regimen and an holding an ongoing loyalty to honesty will forever be required to maintain efficient "reads" from your guidance system.

With that being proposed, here's how readings are acquired...

When you ask a question, the feelings associated with the answer will typically be felt in the solar plexus, originating in the gut, specifically 2 inches right below your navel.

With continued practice in focusing your conscious mind just below the navel and interrogating your brain, you'll eventually develop the ability to sense a very distinct "yes" or "no" when your brain has an obvious, clear answer.

The Big Fucking Secret

You'll sense a "maybe" when your question lacks the specificity required for the brain to produce an assured yes or no, and you'll not sense anything if your question is regarding something in the past, and is unanswerable.

The accuracy in which your emotional guidance system is utilized will accrue as disciplined use persists, and the disease of the mind is increasingly vanquished.

And as you develop a seasoned ability to get "readings", you will even be able to extract an accurate percentage of probability when encountering a maybe[13].

☐ YES
☐ NO
☐ MAYBE
☒ WTF?

Prior to establishing a complete 5th dimensional orientation with reality, your ability to accurately predict the future will be hindered by the disease of the mind, as it has an unfavorable effect on the brain's neurology.

This leads to instances where you must incorporate a degree of conscious discernment to get a proper read...

In some scenarios, the thought (physiologically sensed in and around the head), and the feeling sensed throughout the solar plexus (primarily in the gut) will be contradictory. You may experience an incontrovertible "no" felt around the head, and a "yes" felt around the gut.

In this instance, the gut is always correct.

---

[13] Until you gain the control necessary to psychically read the gut with consistent accuracy, progress may be accelerated through the use of a muscle testing technique.

In other instances, you may have an astounding "yes" in the head and a peculiar "no" in the gut.

This can mean two things...

Either the answer is an astounding "no", or you need to obtain and integrate more information to establish a more exact level of belief in regard to the subject before you make a second attempt.

If the "no" in the gut persists you can typically conclude that the "gut read" is in fact a "no" for the time being.

But if you consciously attempt to honestly integrate all the information you possess, you can potentially activate a 5th dimensional postulate associated with the question at hand, in effect transforming the previous "no" into a "yes".

Belief can successfully eliminate the disease of the mind's effect on your trajectory within the multidimensional matrix.

In extreme cases, the systemic results of the disease of the mind afflicts you in such an extreme manner, that irrational thoughts potentially "trick" your brain into producing a feeling in the body which conveys a message incongruent with reality. Out of control, irrational fear is at the source of this phenomenon.

Granted such a black hole a mysticism is indeed a seemingly perilous state of existence, it can almost always be consciously remedied by pursuing rational objective thought and action, bringing your thoughts back into your control, to be dealt with so your emotional guidance system is again tracking correctly.

The Big Fucking Secret

Rational and objective conscious thought is always at your disposal, and ultimately your only means of living the life you are meant to live.

Responding (not reacting) to Unfavorable Emotions

You'll certainly encounter events you'd presumably deem unfavorable, where things might not transpire the way you had expected. In these instances, you might experience an unfavorable feeling.

統 制

Discipline

While you cannot alter the timing and delivery of emotional sensation in the body, you are in complete control over how you respond to the emotion.

You are in total control of what you think once an emotion is felt, and with your conscious mind, you are responsible for correctly programming the neurology of the brain to benefit from every situation.

For instance, you're a business owner and you get a call from your biggest client. They go on to explain that they have to declare bankruptcy, they can't pay you, and you'll no longer receive their business.

If the business you conduct with this client accounts for 40% of your company's revenue, it most certainly may *seem* like an unfavorable event. As your brain collects that data and integrates the knowledge that this huge portion of your business has suddenly ceased to exist, you would most likely feel an *unfavorable sensation* in the body.

Eli Rook

Yet, as the news of this unfavorable event is being calculated in your brain, the situation transpiring in your life experience at that very moment was solely manifested by you, and you still control the outcome 100%, no matter what you do.

So as a business owner, the response you wield in the face of this seemingly "bad" news has EVERYTHING to do with how destined 5th dimensional postulate continues to render.

If you intend to continue transitioning along the path toward the quantum triangulation of growth and profits, you'll identify the emotions of loss, pain, fear, disappointment, and panic simply as indicators that you need to regain poise (discussed in detail as we explore The Self-Fulfillment Formula in the next chapter).

When your brain triggers an unfavorable feeling in the body, it's not because the event you experienced was "bad". The event is ultimately *irrelevant* to the manifestation of your desires because – if you're increasingly symmetrical – EVERY event you experience is another opportunity to accelerate the rendering of your destined 5th dimensional postulates.

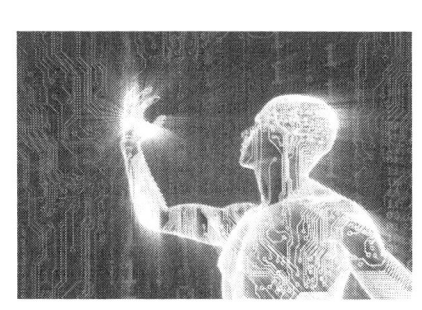

The Big Fucking Secret

Overtime, as you become skilled at immediately and consciously conducting favorable thoughts during the onset of seemingly unfavorable events, you'll eventually find yourself performing the act unconsciously, and the world around you will increasingly change to your favor. Less and less situations and circumstances will catch you off-guard, and you'll become fearless in the face of danger.

**You will be conducting your
life experience as if you are God
(which is how you are meant to live!)**

As you become a master at interpreting the information you receive from you emotional guidance system, you'll use it like a GPS navigation system. You'll respond to an unfavorable emotion objectively, similar to how you'd respond to an advanced traffic warning of a collision along the route you're traveling. You'll simply address your options for alternate routes, and choose the most favorable option to reach your destination.

Just like a response to the objective data you derive from your GPS, the data derived from your emotional guidance system must be objectively observed and responded to with the conscious thoughts which best serve your ongoing pulsation of energy.

It's your pulsation of energy which governs the outcomes you endure, NOT the events transpiring all around you... Your Pulsation is at the <u>SOURCE</u> of EVERYTHING you experience!!

Eli Rook

There are certain degrees of favorability you'll assign to the emotions you feel. You'll feel good or feel bad as you experience emotions, but the emotions are not necessarily good or bad... They're just emotions!

If you can gather one master perspective about emotions from The Big Fucking Secret, it's this...

JUST FEEL THEM!

Feel all the feelings associated with your emotions. Don't cut yourself off from them. Don't suppress them. Don't hide them, or mount guilt for experiencing them.

All Your Feelings
ARE PART OF YOU!

Life is a rich textured canvas you place your unique imprint upon, and emotions are a part of your signature. Experience them, use them for guidance, and respond to their presence rationally.

What is the ideal emotional state for maintaining conscious control of existence for the increased happiness of yourself and others?

The answer to this question is ultimately FEELING GOOD.

Every emotion will have a degree of favorability, and how you think will determine what emotions you experience, but ultimately the best conditions for happiness thinking in a way that provides and endless flow of GOOD FEELINGS.

And while there are an almost endless number of activities you can perform to feel good, you own personal thoughts are always the immediate source through which evoke good feeling emotions.

The Big Fucking Secret

Feeling good tunes your Pulsation to match the frequency of The All, establishing harmony, and conducting energy into your life which is congruent with your nature - the innate purpose you serve as a conscious being - the responsibility of being HAPPY.

The challenge you'll endure as you experience quantum crossings into a 5th dimensional orientation with reality is AWARENESS of emotions tied to irrational thought.

Constantly monitoring your emotional guidance system and consciously executing effort to the think and act rationally and objectively is the task at hand.

When you notice yourself drifting away from the state of feeling good, your awareness of the drift serves as an indicator that you need to restore consciousness of the fact that you are God – an important element in The Self-Fulfillment Formula, which we can now delve into.

In preparation for the next chapter, consider putting the book down and take an hour to do something that makes you feel exceedingly good =)

Eli Rook

The Big Fucking Secret

Eli Rook

CHAPTER 8

In the upcoming Alpha Version of The Big Fucking Secret, Chapter 8 will fully outline The Self-Fulfillment formula, the Three Fundamental Modalities, the Gamma Wave Induction & Pineal Activation techniques; as well as a rundown of various common denominators in your ongoing self-fulfillment.

Aside from a few key elements, The Self-Fulfillment Formula is nothing new, and has been described at great length in countless books throughout history.

It's a formula you've UNCONSCIOUSLY used to create all the favorable results you've experienced throughout your life... And the reason for illustrating this apparent formula is ultimately to assist you using the formula CONSCIOUSLY.

You'll notice as you've been reading this final rough draft / final beta version of The Big Fucking Secret, there's been no mention of techniques or protocols of any kind, aside from the constant suggestion that a thriving life is largely due to the control of one's own thoughts.

As there are hundreds and thousands of books which detail techniques and ways of going about achieving self-fulfillment, it's the aim of The Big Fucking Secret to condense the entire realm of essential factors disseminated from those books (in less than 20 pages).

But due to the progress made on this final rough draft as the pending publishing deadline nears, Chapter 8 is being omitted.

The Big Fucking Secret

While this may disappoint some readers, the fact stands that every reader already knows everything about what they need to do in life to thrive.

The ultimate "secret of all secrets" can be summed up in three words: "You are God." And it's ultimately to which degree you fully understand this concept that your thoughts and actions will produce the results you wish to transpire.

The unique offering brought forth by "The Big Fucking Secret" is that it induces quantum crossings into a 5th dimensional orientation with reality, expressing what you already know in an ascended light. *It's the energy from the authors' vantage point, in a 5th dimensional orientation with reality, which is conducted through the words you read, delivering the effects you experience while reading.*

Yet, the technical details in Chapter 8 will certainly add fuel to the benefits you create in your life having experienced this 5th dimensional ascension.

The final rough draft / final beta version of The Big Fucking Secret you now hold will be on the market for a very short period of time. It has been modestly priced, and due to it's limited distribution, the potential for profitable resale in the years to come is a benefit to all who possess a copy.

The Alpha Version will be the next in order, presumably followed by Theta, Delta, Beta2, and an eventual Gamma Version. The omission of Chapter 8 at this time does not inhibit the quantum crossings you'll experience from reading the book in the manner suggested, so forge onward. For updates on the latest releases and newest developments of this "living book", subscribe at BigFuckingSecret.com

Eli Rook

The Big Fucking Secret

CHAPTER 9

How free do you feel knowing that you've ultimately been at the source of all your success?

In those moments throughout your life, while you were so determined to reach your goal, when a random event sealed your success at the very last minute – you did that!

And when you were in the depths of despair, having no choice but to focus all of your energy toward getting back to where you wanted to be – it was YOU who turned it all around!

You've been using your mind, brain, and body to channel "source energy" into power, and you've been using that power to bring forth all that you fear and desire into your life experience.

You've always been in total control of your existence... to your betterment *and* to your detriment.

You've been consciously manifesting specific outcomes in your life experience by coding programs into the multidimensional matrix and navigating the situations and circumstances you encountered.

You've referred to this phenomenon as:
"Making a decision and following through to the end - no matter what!"

The Big Fucking Secret

You've also been consciously creating experiences reflecting everything you fear and everything you don't want, commonly referred to as "WORRYING", or "expecting bad things to happen".

Now you understand the value of practicing the proper use of your technology, consciously focusing on your destined fifth dimensional postulates and using your feelings as a guide to bring your pulsation of energy into symmetry with who you are meant to be.

You become, or get, what you think about most of the time because you program The All to render the sum of your thoughts from moment to moment, from thought to thought.

change your thoughts and you change your world.

While you have all the basic information you need to render specific think your desire into your life experience, dedicated practice is required to establish a complete 5th dimensional orientation with reality, so the immediacy in which you manifest a desire is automatically unleashed without conscious effort.

The momentum of growing confidence and increasing power you acquire through continued success helps you expand what you believe to be possible, and manifest results with increasing accuracy in time. The results you increasingly see provide greater levels of comfort, control, creativity, intuition, health, motivation, and bliss in your daily life, thus delivering a more automatic awareness of the fact that you are God as your life persists.

Three Fundamental Modalities

You must REMEMBER information in order to use it, and you must USE information in order to see RESULTS.

Committing these three elements to memory and use them in your life with repetition until they become PART OF YOU, permanently hardwired into the brain.

1. *Attain the full awareness that YOU ARE GOD and take 100% responsibility for everything you experience*

2. *Think about what you're thinking about and change what you're thinking to be aligned with the manifestation of your desires.*

3. *Sustain poise, perform the right activities required for ongoing success.*

If you want to be a master, you must become a relentless student and practitioner of information around the subject of success.

That means immersing yourself in study *daily*, while consistently exerting effort and discipline toward being who you are meant to be *all the time*.

The Big Fucking Secret

Your default to operate under the direction of your hypothalamus enables the persistence of an evolutionary-driven "survival mode" to dominate your thinking.

In this survival mode, your brain scans the fifth dimension for unfavorable outcomes derived from your illusions of fear and scarcity, then commands The All to deliver experiences reflecting all which you do not want.

Throughout your life, your brain has been programmed (by you) to be a submissive, irresponsible blueprint by which nature's automatic operating system designs an intricate labyrinth of unfavorable situations and circumstances (which you have the option of navigating toward your eventual death).

But as you come into greater awareness of the fact that you are God, you turning away from disappointment, disease, and death – toward happiness, health, and helping others. The quantum crossings your endure into a new world bring forth a quality of life that markedly improves.

Your awakening to the full realization that you are God is the quintessential breakthrough that frees you from the shackles of nature's evolutionary meat grinder, which all unconscious lifeforms are subject to.

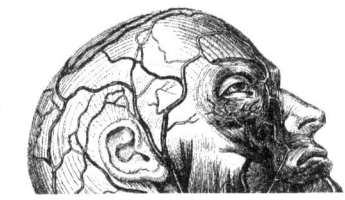

As you harness more power and harmonize the pulsation of energy you emit, you use that power to consciously control existence to your favor; which builds confidence.

The state of confidence you experience in the mind can be used to fuel further effort to exert more conscious control of existence, fulfilling your life purpose to a greater extent, bringing you into greater symmetry with The All.

The rolling momentum you experience as the power flows into your life through this process catapults you to experience more complex manifestations of SUCCESS.

With that being known, an indicator of your failure to maintain the effort required to experience success is your sudden LOSS OF POWER.

The Big Fucking Secret

A loss of power is immediately noticed in your physiological feelings, and almost always occurs as a result of your thought process in conflict with the fact that you are by nature 100% responsibility for everything you experience.

Those who are conscious of their defaults, and consciously correct defaults with speed and consistency, generally "bounce back" from a loss of power with little time lost.

Those unconscious of their mistakes, and possessing no knowledge of how to use their technology to fix the dire experiences they face, could certainly spiral downward into depression or worse.

No matter how deep the depression or how far the downward spiral might take you away from the life you were meant to live, the remedy is always the same:

The Three Fundamental Modalities

1. Restore consciousness of the fact that you are God and take 100% responsibility for everything you experience.

2. Think about what you're thinking about and change what you think about to support the manifestation of your desires.

3. And sustain poise, performing the right activities to continue producing success.

Eli Rook

While focused on taking action to manifest the outcome you desire, you will from time to time have a tendency to feel frustration, fear, anger, and a host of emotions which might lead you to assume you are not producing success.

Note that those emotions are NOT signs of impending failure... They're simply indicating your need to revisit the three fundamental modalities.

Once you successfully launch a program into The All, it's stuck there until it expires... If you follow The Self-Fulfillment Formula, the specific postulate you program into the field will NEVER EXPIRE.

So the only way you can stop the program from manifesting your desire is either by consciously canceling it, generating resistance (doubt), or not producing the necessary effort for it to fully render.

Not exerting the necessary effort, or not properly eliminating the resistance you face will inevitably lead to a drift away from symmetry, losing power and consciousness of the fact that you are God.

If left unchecked, such a default will surely guarantee your descent into a whirlpool of unfavorable circumstances and situations.

The Big Fucking Secret

You have the tools to control what renders in your life experience. Your physiology provides the guidance system to assist you knowing which way to go, and your brain is commanding the entire existence field to bend to your will.

Keep in mind, as your power grows, and you increasingly master higher degrees of conscious control, the stakes continuously rise, obstacles continuously mount, and your ascent to mastery is continuously challenged.

Such is the nature of the game we play.

You'll stand up, get knocked down, and get back up, but you'll in a state of "perpetual becoming"... Becoming more of who you're meant to be along the ups and down of this ride called life.

There's no end to this road you're on. There's no final destination... Just an endless array of lush potentiality available for your consumption. You'll always be in the hot seat to experience MORE.

Use what you know to become who you feel you should be, and affect the world around you to reflect what you believe it can become.

As you change, the world around you changes.

Allow us to repeat this again so you may consider the

ramifications of such a statement with greater depth and understanding...

As you change, the world around you changes.

This is not a phenomena that will occur sometime in the distant future... It's not fantasy... It's reality. It's happening in REAL-TIME.

Your total ongoing cognition of the three fundamental modalities, and your mastery of The Self-Fulfillment Formula will mark the end of your voluntary isolation in the Exo-God slave-yard, and the final quantum crossing into a 5th dimensional orientation with reality.

So take inventory... Are you living every moment with the characteristics of someone who is fully aware of the fact that they are God?

The Big Fucking Secret

CHAPTER 10

What do people living with the full realization that they are God experience from day to day?

What can you expect now that you hold the same cognition they hold?

Those who are fully conscious of the fact they are God experience deep internal happiness. You can feel their happiness just by being in their presence.

They have good posture, they're pleasant to be around, and they can look you in the eye when you speak to them.

They have POISE.

They are AT PEACE.

They are in CONTROL.

They are consumed with love.

You'll never hear someone exhibiting poise MAKE EXCUSES about why they didn't do something. They ALWAYS take 100% responsibility for EVERYTHING they experience.

You'll never hear someone exhibiting poise sharing negative commentary about existence, or speaking in terms of doubt and fear about existence. They never speak in a manner of limited means. They always speak with creative force aimed at building dreams, not destroying them.

The Big Fucking Secret

Can you imagine someone literally jumping up out of bed every morning, eyes wide as saucers, because the exhilaration of another amazing day to create more of their dreams finally arrived?

Those who live in total harmony with who-they-were-meant-to-be have the ability to live each day with boundless energy.

They wake up and start each day with enthusiasm because they understand they're IN THE PROCESS of making their dreams come true. They have an obsession with the fun exciting projects they're working on. They have positive anticipation for all the good things that will happen throughout the day.

Who you desire to be and what type of day you desire to have is 100% under your control. How you assess the good and bad things in life is 100% your choice. You are in total control of your experience, regardless of the opinions and perceptions of those around you.

Who you were meant to be is someone actively spinning the vortex of life, not being spun about through nature's discretion. Who you were meant to be absolutely LOVES the work you do, and wakes up every morning excited that your body and brain are recharged, and ready to enjoy the process of rendering your 5th dimensional postulates throughout another challenging and rewarding day.

Eli Rook
You smile more!

The smile on your face will come deep from within because you feel lighter, you feel content, you feel good knowing EVERYTHING is ultimately working out to your advantage in ways you aren't even aware of.

You walk faster. You have better posture. Your muscles relax and tension leaves your body. *You feel comfortable in your skin everywhere you go.*

When you walk, talk, sit, and stand - while surrounded by others, and even in solitude - you emit the pulsation of God.

You not only notice your own mental, emotional, and physiological changes taking place, but you increasingly notice these changes taking place in those around you.

When you do happen to notice the ways others around you are not changing you understand this observation is completely natural in the beginning. The dynamics of life NEVER frustrate someone who has attained POISE.

All individuals change at the pace which is perfect for them - and some choose never to change!

Whatever others decide to do with their own time and their own lives - at their own pace - is 100% OK with you.

The Big Fucking Secret

As God, you eagerly offer your good will, enthusiasm, and loving intentions to those you come in contact with, because you know they'll surely become who they were meant to be in whatever time frame best suits them.

You certainly care about others and celebrate their desires, and you certainly consider giving aid to those who request your assistance, but you always give them the gift of finding their own way toward who they are meant to be, even if you decide to share your wisdom.

Even as a teacher of this knowledge, you never wish to remain in the presence of those who swim against the stream of intention. Such individuals certainly pose as helpful reminders you've gone off course. Simply swim around them and proceed in the direction of the current. Experiencing their presence only makes you stronger, forcing you to FOCUS.

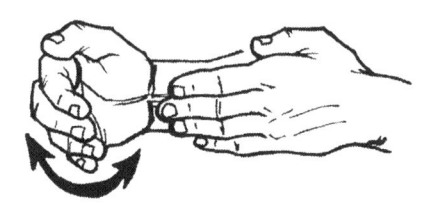

The degree of ease in which you maneuver through The All is 100% under your control, and to whose favor you control reality is 100% your responsibility.

With the anticipation of being challenged while developing an awareness of the fact that you are God around those who are not, you might ponder who you should associate with and who you should learn from.

**You might ask,
"Who do I listen to?"**

Eli Rook

While this book may have taken you to the core of honesty and helped you piece together the puzzle of who you really are, you might be content in knowing all you know now, and continue to create a life of fulfillment with very little study of additional material.

Conversely, you may be hungry to figure out how the knowledge you possess integrates with the wide spectrum of other teachings made available throughout the ages.

There's a chance you possess parasitic neural pathways in the brain blocking your ability to turn away from the old world of Exo-God and step into the new illuminating world illustrated in this book, so you must at all costs reconcile any potential mythology you've developed throughout your life.

With no surprise, you'll quickly find the majority of modern teachers, gurus, and authors are still convinced that they are not God!

And as you can imagine, when you're explicitly following the instructions of people who believe reality works in a way that it does not, you most likely will create results reflecting the degree of misalignment embedded in their instructions.

This does not mean you can't enjoy success following the instructions of individuals who are still convinced they're not God... Indeed, you can still learn from others regardless of their conceptual flaws.

The Big Fucking Secret

Using your skills of discernment, you eagerly open yourself up to be able to process and utilize ALL knowledge without resistance or bias.

As God, you accept the fact there is SO MUCH you don't know, and so much MORE to learn about everything you already do know, you MUST BE in a perpetual state of learning, discerning, and integrating knowledge – even when you *think* you already know the TRUTH.

THIS IS IMPORTANT!

You've experienced a lifetime of self-deception under the illusion that you are not God...

Be weary of what you think the "truth" really is.

As you approach scientific studies, philosophical studies, religious studies, economic studies, and you review information provided by schools, companies, organizations, individuals... even cults – you'll best seek out exactly what you need to know by capturing the ENTIRE SPECTRUM of knowledge you encounter *(not merely a closed off corner of knowledge, such as that found in many of the before mentioned categories and institutions)*.

BUT BEWARE OF GETTING STUCK IN LEARNING MODE! I ASSURE YOU... YOU HAVE GREATNESS WITHIN YOU AND YOU HAVE ACCESS TO ALL THE KNOWLEDGE YOU NEED <u>RIGHT</u> <u>NOW</u> TO DO WHAT YOU WERE MEANT TO DO. Yes, you need to be a perpetual student for ongoing success, but also know that you can begin seeing results RIGHT NOW.

Eli Rook

Throughout the history of conscious life on planet Earth, those who mastered the art of consciously controlling existence systematically codified their methods, and for millenia, handed down their information from generation to generation.

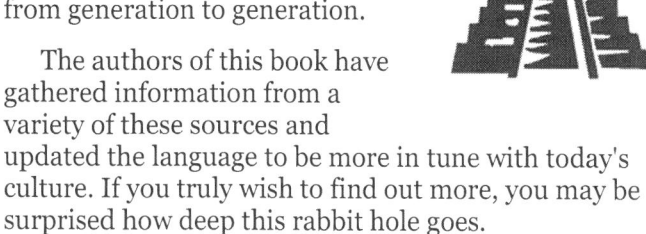

The authors of this book have gathered information from a variety of these sources and updated the language to be more in tune with today's culture. If you truly wish to find out more, you may be surprised how deep this rabbit hole goes.

There are advanced techniques for controlling existence, such as recoding physical matter so it appears differently to other conscious beings, molding energy into vortices to energize other conscious beings for the purpose of healing, mating, and cooperation, changing the energetic charge of physical location, and very real things you would think were science fiction had you not first experienced the power of being conscious that you are God, or physically witnessing the acts of those who have mastered the use of their technology!

You will certainly learn more techniques as you increasingly cross into a 5th dimensional orientation, change your DNA, and improve your ability to control existence.

The Big Fucking Secret

One power-multiplying technique is achieved by physically connecting your mind with the minds of one or more conscious individuals in a live physical setting, forming a single "mastermind[14]".

Imagine you were one of the fully charged batteries in a flash light, but you were nudged in between a pair of batteries whose storage of power had been depleted.

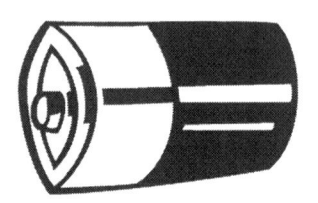

Your capacity alone to successfully illuminate the bulb would be null, but when you find yourself between a pair of fully charged batteries, you may easily fulfill the task.

This is not unlike the dynamics found in life where the creation of a certain outcome requires a team of conscious beings working in unison.

To manifest certain outcomes it may take the conscious power of one conscious being to give birth to an idea, but it takes an army of conscious beings to create the physical manifestation of that idea in The All.

---

[14] The scientific nature of the "mastermind" was first widely publicly described in Napoleon Hill's first book "The Law of Success in 16 Lessons"

Eli Rook

Consider a skyscraper. The conscious effort required to complete the physical manifestation of a skyscraper goes far beyond one conscious being in control of existence... It requires hundreds.

When associating with like-minded conscious beings and working together in a harmonious fashion, the grouping of minds AMPLIFIES the power of each individual mind, therefore amplifying the intensity of the commands emitted into The All. Plus, just spending time being around people who have already become wildly successful doing all the things you want to do has a permanent effect on you.

- Maybe you want access to vast amounts of physical and financial capital...

- Maybe you want to achieve a greater level of health where you feel great every day.

- Maybe you just want to have more happiness, adventure, and excitement in your life.

- *(Maybe you want to help others by giving more and contributing more to your community.)*

If these are things you desire, you can surely experience them using the information presented in this book. But regularly being around other like-minded people who *already* achieved financial freedom, vibrant health, travel the world, and engage in philanthropic activities *dramatically accelerates* your ability to do those things yourself... (Talking to them on the internet does not.)

The Big Fucking Secret

A proverbial saying goes, "Five years from now your income will be the average of your five best friends."

Just as well, five years from now your happiness and health will be the average of your five best friends!

Five years from now the number of people you'll be able to serve on this planet will probably be the average number of people your five best friends are able to serve.

It's dramatically easier to do things you've just begun to practice after seeing others do them with greater skill than your own.

You simply do not get access to the information you need, or the experiences you need, being an isolated individual whose only connection to other like-minded people is through the internet.

If you'd like to experience this phenomena, your next move is in the direction of finding other like-minded people who understand what you understand.

Physically associating and "masterminding" with other like-minded individuals has immense productive benefits that enable you to accelerate the manifestation of your desires.

Ideally you should seek out joining an organization that celebrates the principles shared in books like The Big Fucking Secret. This could be a business organization, a charitable foundation, or an activity-oriented association.

Eli Rook

The authors of this book and many of the readers who enjoy its contents belong to several different organizations that are focused on self improvement.

Visit **BigFuckingSecret.com** to find out more.

Wherever you're located on Planet Earth, you can physically make contact with others who are headed in the direction you're headed.

You are not an island.

You're one with all existence.

Connect. Create. Change your world.

Make all your drams come true, and help others do the same.

The Big Fucking Secret

CHAPTER 11

With the cognition that you are God, and your focus on mastering the ability to consciously control existence in your favor, you may wonder what will happen on planet Earth as you increasingly triangulate into the Civilization of Luminiferous Ascension.

Conscious beings exist throughout existence, and there are an endless number of conscious civilizations throughout the multiverse.

Throughout existence, lifeforms spring forth from nature, evolve to become increasingly intelligent, and eventually harness consciousness to control existence. They then harness greater power to establish conditions in which conscious life may continue to evolve.

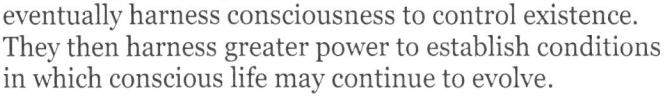

Other civilizations throughout existence have been conscious for tens of thousands, hundreds of thousands, millions, *even billions of years*, or more... while our civilization is estimated to have only been conscious for the last three thousand years or so.

Still in our infancy, where do you think our civilization is headed as more and more individuals discover the big fucking secret?

The Big Fucking Secret

As we've been evolving biologically throughout the past, our ability to learn how to utilize technology has been driving the advancement of our species, enabling us to increasingly reach greater survival milestones in shorter amounts of time.

Throughout history we've used technology as an extension of our physical existence to rationally expedite our evolutionary development.

For instance, over an eon ago, the technology of fire was regularly used to cook meat, aiding the human digestive system in breaking down certain enzymes, which over time, accelerated the growth of the brain, making way for advancements in cognitive thought and language, which then led to our ability to harness consciousness.

Later, the technology of the wheel was used to harness power in transporting physical matter, increasing the efficacy individuals achieved in life-sustaining aspects of agriculture and trade.

Nearly 600 years ago, the technology of the printing press caused an explosion of intelligence due to the mass availability of books, spurring the renaissance of the 17th century, and later the enlightenment of the 18th century.

Eli Rook

At the turn of the 19th century, the technology of the steam locomotive brought the potential for high speed mobility across vast geographic areas, boosting the discovery of natural resources, dramatically increasing domestic and international trade, and enabling the rapid expansion of entirely new industries – which in turn caused the standard of living amongst the working class to skyrocket.

In the 20th century we witnessed technology enhancing the existence of conscious beings with greater life sustaining force than ever before.

We observed the humble beginnings of electricity, then automobiles, telephones, airplanes, mass industrialization, then computers, space travel, satellite technology, the internet, and biotechnology...

We see a pattern of technology increasingly becoming more widespread and more accessible to more individuals, delivering overwhelming NET benefits to all conscious beings.

Child mortality rates have dramatically decreased on every continent. Human beings are living longer lives in greater comfort than ever before. The use of technology has been instrumental in toppling dictatorial governments, abandoning life-suppressing religions, and rejecting the false authority of an elite ruling class.

The Big Fucking Secret

Now technology is being harnessed to sustain life beyond the unforgiving pressures of nature with biotechnology, nanotechnology, and robotics, eventually leading us to harness control over nature's most daunting limitation – DEATH.

It's nature's evolutionary system of renewal that allows patterns of biological death to affect unconscious lifeforms, but with our consciousness of the fact that we are God, we're increasingly taking control over our own evolution, in effect accelerating evolution to overcome the limitations of our biological housing.

Similar to that achieved by advanced conscious civilizations throughout existence, humanity's ultimate milestone of creative intelligence will be to build non-aging biological bodies for conscious beings on planet Earth who wish to sustain their current life experience indefinitely.

As stewards of our planet and our species, it's our duty to clean up the backlash of the industrial age, establish peaceful, flourishing free enterprise environments upon borderless lands, and sustain every last precious conscious life wishing to reside in this beautiful new world.

Eli Rook

At the time of this book's publication, conscious beings are eradicating the criminal element thriving within the governmental and corporate structures of the world, rapidly developing technology to deliver free decentralized sources of energy to everyone on the planet, and successfully fixing the legacy issues within human biology.

Due to exponential growth in all technologies, game changing breakthroughs are occurring across all industries, effecting all aspects of society.

Digital communications and new media are enabling the spread of awareness and fueling new means of commerce. Cheap personal recording devices and the semantic web are beginning to converge to form a matrix of honesty through which individuals in positions of leadership will be held accountable.

Photo-cellular storage capacity is growing exponentially, putting the cost of generating solar power equal to the cost of generating power from fossil fuels, by the mid 2010's.

Alternative monetary technologies are springing forth to provide solutions in the face of unstable, debt-driven fiat currencies.

The Big Fucking Secret

With technological advancements in biotechnology, nanotechnology, and robotics, it's estimated that therapies to slow the speed of cellular aging will be commercially available by 2020, reverse aging technologies available by the year 2029, and commercial biological immortality affordable to the masses by the year 2045.

It is statistically probable that if you're under the age of 50 years old today, in excellent health, you will most certainly have access to biotechnological cellular rejuvenation therapies which slow, cease, then eventually reverse the effects of aging endured by the body – expanding your lifetime by hundreds, thousands, and eventually millions of years.

More advanced technologies such as mind uploading via quantum computing and "soul transfer" to flesh and blood, semi-robotic "backup" bodies is on the horizon well within this century. *(You'll want to ensure the work you do, and the relationships you establish on planet Earth, persist uninterrupted, for as long as you desire.)*

(Access the video archive at BigFuckingSecret.com to learn more about the above mentioned subjects.)

Eli Rook

These rapidly advancing technologies will come about whether or not the majority of individuals on planet Earth choose to engage in their use.

We're witnessing the progression of a civilization destined to manifest a mode of existence its cosmic immortal contemporaries consider commonplace.

The new world is here whether or not the majority of conscious individuals realize it or not.

Just as we're still not 100% sure about the missing puzzle pieces of our evolutionary past, puzzle pieces of the future will fall into place as we forge onward.

We command the favorable outcomes we experience as we go, and just knowing you're the determining force transforming life on this planet, you should light up with fierce enthusiasm and determination.

You have The Self-Fulfillment Formula. You understand how your mind, brain, and body work. You understand how you interface with the existence field, and you're fully aware that you control existence.

You understand your purpose on planet Earth, which is to enjoy happiness and contribute to the happiness of others. You understand that all your fears and all your desires are manifesting *in real time*, and you have 100% control over everything you experience (you always have, and you always will).

The Big Fucking Secret

You have a perspective of history, the future, and how every particle in existence is in motion RIGHT NOW in your life experience rendering the perfect match to your pulsation of energy.

You can have, be, or do anything and everything you want, and as you reach greater symmetry with who you're meant to be, the child of the past inside you becomes more and more eager to come out and play – so let's play!

Eli Rook

The Big Fucking Secret

CONCLUSION

Are you enjoying your quantum crossings?

You were instructed to read The Big Fucking Secret cover-to-cover, and then read it cover-to-cover once more.

Do you feel good knowing you have access to the information you need, and the power within yourself to take control of your own evolution?

You'll undoubtedly read this book more than two times, but do consider sticking to your commitment, finish reading the following ILLUMINATIONS, and then proceed to re-read the entire book cover-to-cover.

Fearlessly stand before the vortex of existence and now know that everything you ever loved and ever wanted to transpire in your life is now rushing toward you. You have no more blockages, no more resistance, and things are happening in ways you cannot even comprehend to serve your conscious command.

The Big Fucking Secret

From an individual's first cognition of the fact that they are God, it may be a matter of weeks or months during which they zoom toward the full realization they are God, take 100% responsibility for everything happening in their lives, and consciously control reality in their favor to experience dramatically improved conditions.

Other individuals who experience the new cognition that they are God might take *months*, or sometimes YEARS, before they really begin to consciously control reality in their favor with consistency.

The speed at which one can enjoy all the physical and emotional benefits of being fully conscious of the fact that they are God is based on the individual's investment of time and effort.

No one magically transformed into a powerful, competent conscious controller of existence overnight. It requires a burning desire, passionate determination, and a relentless decision to go for it.

You now hold in your mind everything you need to make progress. Your brain has been permanently reprogrammed by reading this book, and you'll find, as you read it again, it will seem like an entirely new book... That's because your brain is now able to perform wider integrations, and you're able to enjoy new cognitions about how you control existence as you manifest all of your desires.

Eli Rook

So continue traveling into greater symmetry with who you are meant to be, and enjoy total clarity in the thriving Civilization of Luminiferous Ascension!

With a burning desire and love in your heart, you're eternally bound for greatness.

                                              Blessings,

                                              Eli

The Big Fucking Secret

Eli Rook

ILLUMINATIONS

Civilization of Luminiferous Ascension

The Civilization of Luminiferous Ascension (the Civilization of the Universe, Kingdom of God, etc.) is a very real civilization where poverty, hunger, crime, disease, and death on planet Earth do not exist.

You have "instant download access" to this Civilization, and you have the ability to <u>fully</u> render this Civilization on planet Earth in your current life experience.

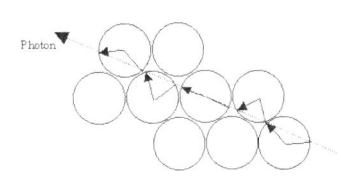

Throughout your consciousness experience, while each subsequent Planck unit of existence is encountered, you continuously transition along a trajectory of precise quantum positions.

You're <u>ALWAYS</u> on a trajectory toward the CLA.

Your pulsation of energy is solely responsible for governing your navigation along the perpetual trajectory toward the CLA. But the disease of the mind slightly alters your trajectory, prohibiting an optimum course.

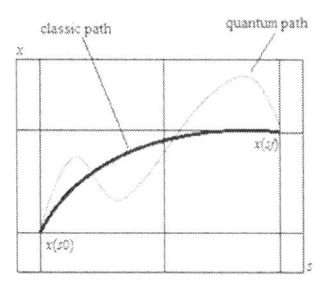

The Big Fucking Secret

An array of endless onmidimensional "alternate realities" simultaneous co-exist "alongside" your life experience on planet Earth. And as you traverse your quantum trajectory toward the CLA, your ability to cure the disease of the mind optimizes the course of your trajectory, more speedily rendering the CLA in your life experience.

The Civilization of Luminiferous Ascension exists in a frequency range just beyond the normal frequency range you've "tuned into" on planet Earth, throughout most of your current life experience.

At any time, you may "tune in" to the frequency range of the CLA and incorporate its frequencies into your Pulsation, more speedily rendering the CLA in your life experience... But being convinced that such a simple manner of function isn't possible *prohibits* your ability to optimize your trajectory toward fully entrenched quantum positions in the CLA!

The Big Fucking Secret provides the foundational concept through which you will ultimately tighten your course toward the new world, engaging in a complete quantum crossing from a 4th dimensional orientation with reality into a 5th dimensional orientation with reality, so the CLA may fully render all around you.

Eli Rook
Alternate Realities

"Alternate Realities" is an inaccurate term describing the co-existence of your residual self-image endlessly scattered throughout the multidimensional matrix, but the term is valuable in its metaphorical expression of how other conscious beings experience alternate versions of you, which are uniquely customized to persist in their life experiences.

To conceptualize the metaphorical value of the term, imagine that in 10 years, you completely render the CLA on planet Earth in your life experience, and all the conscious beings on the planet enjoy a prosperous, safe, co-existence, where all wars have ended, technology soars, and the basic needs of human beings are met and exceeded.

Imagine the rendering of your closest friends experiencing the exhilaration of this new world right along with you...

Now imagine that in 10 years, you fully render a living hell on planet Earth, where suffering, disease, and death are all around you, and the ultimate extinction of the human species is probabilistically destined.

The Big Fucking Secret

Now let us hypothetically propose that the entire realm of potentiality you have access to may only result in you experiencing only one of those two worlds, and nothing more. Understand both worlds already exist within the multidimensional matrix... Yet the life experience you encounter in one, or the other, will render based on your Pulsation.

And here's the paradigm you must grasp about the nature of these "alternate realities"...

If you fully render the CLA in 10 years, the individual conscious beings conducting their existence into your life experience will think, speak, and act in a manner which is consistent with the stimulating, liberating free world you live in... But if you fully render hell on Earth in 10 years, the individual conscious beings conducting their existence into your life experience will think, speak, and act in a manner which is consistent with the devastating limitations and worldwide decline into extinction.

Now understand that YOUR residual self-image accessed by other individual conscious beings will be custom-tailored to the parameters in which THEIR life experience persists.

To bring this illustration into even more light, consider that, right now, there's an "alternate reality" here on planet Earth where martial law has been enacted, dozens of wars are being conducted simultaneously on every continent, global food shortages are causing billions to barely survive, and entire cities have been leveled by nuclear assault.

Eli Rook

*Fortunately, you did not
render such a scenario!*

You are SOLELY responsible for the life experience you render. You have been since you became conscious, and you always will be.

Facing this paradigm, everyone on planet Earth who intends on surviving will take responsibility for everything happening in their lives, and change the world they live in so it reflects the optimum conditions available within the 5th dimension of potentiality.

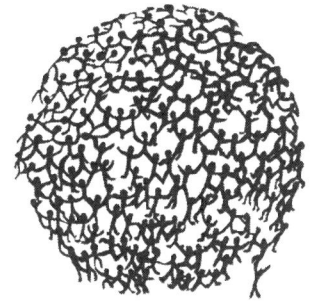

As you take such a position and tighten your trajectory toward the CLA, you'll realize the most glorious new world you could ever imagine is actually RIGHT THERE on the horizon, and it's barreling forward upon the dictum of your will.

The Good News

The good news is you've already partially "downloaded" the CLA in your life experience. You witness many of its characteristics all around you, such as high technology, honest business, spontaneous healing, storybook romance, thrilling artistic feats, etc.

Liken the "download" speed you're experiencing to the speed in which you would download a 1 megabyte photo on a 56k dial-up modem. At 56k, it could take up to a few minutes for a picture to download, only revealing a small portion of the photo as each few seconds pass. But on a high-speed broadband connection, that 1 megabyte image renders almost instantaneously.

The Big Fucking Secret

In complete 5d immersion, the CLA renders instantaneously... and it does so without regard to the hardware being used. The only variable in speed is ultimately the degree of accuracy honed by the user in establishing a connection.

Events and Time

The speed in which you render the CLA is based on the laws of physics, as they optimize your access to potentiality from the fifth dimension, and the degree in which your Pulsation is harmonized with the frequency of the CLA.

Consider that A) It takes time to cure the disease of the mind and B) Events you would rather not encounter will certainly happen along your path to mental health.

Early 21st Century Earth is certainly a carnival of perilous dangers, but proceeding with an unwavering resolve in your control of reality will increasingly move you into a protective field where you bypass negative circumstances any external event may pose.

As you continue to establish an unobstructed cognition that you are God, you will eventually reach a point where you experience very few negative events, even if you have not fully rendered the CLA.

When the pulsation of energy you emit into The All becomes symmetrical with who you were meant to be in the CLA, The All bends to deliver winning streak after winning streak into your life.

Eli Rook

How long does it take to reach the point in your life where everything works out to your advantage - as if by magic?

The answer is "How much time are you willing to invest practicing?", "How much money are you willing to invest exploring?", and "How much effort are you willing to invest traveling to where you want to go?"

Ascension is a <u>LIFESTYLE</u>.

The Big Fucking Secret was designed to help you perform a complete overhaul on your thinking in only two short readings. But that's all it offers... An overhaul.

You'll become the person you were meant to be by organizing a LIFESTYLE around becoming that person.

And once you become that person, the lifestyle will never change; because you'll forever be in the pursuit of greater ascension.

Ultimately, it takes <u>TIME</u>.

By engaging in your ability to control existence in your favor, and mastering your ability to achieve accurate preferable results, you'll eventually have the cognition that everything is happening in the perfect way, at the perfect time, in order for everything you want to transpire – even when it seems like it's not.

The Big Fucking Secret
Taking Responsibility

In the early stages it may seem challenging to take responsibility for EVERYTHING that happens to you.

You'll observe an event as being completely out of your control - like being late to the airport, and missing your flight.

Then you'll ponder how your pulsation of energy is interacting with The All, and how the events you experience are all being organized to best reflect your deepest fears and desires along a timeline to render your destined 5th dimensional postulates.

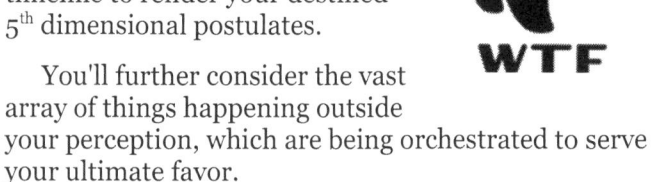

You'll further consider the vast array of things happening outside your perception, which are being orchestrated to serve your ultimate favor.

Only by rejecting the fact that you are responsible for everything happening in your life experience will you manage to let an unfavorable event lead to your command of an additional unfavorable event.

Justice

A criminal element has certainly existed throughout your life experience on planet Earth, and you certainly may face situations and circumstances where this criminal element could pose a threat to you prior to your complete transition into a 5th dimensional orientation with reality.

If an individual violates the individual rights of another, shouldn't that individual be brought to justice?

Guilty parties in a crime, or parties responsible for a violation of your individual rights should certainly be held accountable, but to what extent you pursue reparations is a personal preference, and cannot be based on objective standards.

From a 5th dimensional orientation, every unjust act you personally experience is ultimately your own fault, yet from a 4th dimensional orientation you are the victim of every unjust act.

A conundrum such as this can only be permanently resolved by curing the disease of the mind.

Curing the disease of the mind shifts the quantum triangulation of all the other conscious beings whose life experience intersects your own, allowing justice to be embedded within all the transactions they conduct.

Until you achieve complete immersion in the Civilization of the Luminiferous Ascension, consider that your sustained symmetrical pulsation of energy, and your physical efforts to fulfill your life's purpose, actively vanishes the criminal element on planet Earth in ways which are not always objectively evident.

The Big Fucking Secret
Civilization

From some perspectives, it may *seem* as if civilization is in decline!

Sometimes we find ourselves in perilous situations from which it *seems* impossible to escape.

When all the facts point to a mass system failure, you have no choice but to rationally prepare yourself for the worst, and believe everything will somehow work out to your advantage.

Feel good knowing the pressure to fix problems we face is a recurring element in life which has always historically yielded a *shift* toward victory (and it always will.)

Shift *yourself* to participate in this grand fluctuation toward more favorable experiences in life.

You

Your increasing symmetry with who you were meant to be causes systemic positive effects on every other conscious being you connect with. *The pursuit of your best life cleanses the entire realm of existence through which your life experience is conducted.*

You illuminate the cosmos with the gift of your Pulsation, and the further you spread your light, the more all those conducting intersecting life experiences with your own may ascend.

Eli Rook

The ultimate imperative in getting the most out of using The Big Fucking Secret is maintaining a consistent awareness of the fact that you are God.

If you are going through life convinced you are not God, or existing under illusions that you do not control existence, ALL your thought processes are stifled with an aberrant foundational conceptualization about reality, which contradicts your nature as a conscious being.

The contradiction you maintain against your nature as a conscious being is what restricts you from being who you are meant to be.

Consciousness & Nature's Coexistence

All lifeforms manifest their own unique life experience by way of nature's automatic operating system. Conscious beings are set apart from nature's automatic operating system, as they use consciousness to manifest a life experience *in tandem* with nature.

The advent of consciousness is a phenomenon apart from nature, as it exists in a capacity where nature's spirit must come to know itself and conduct a life experience beyond the constraints of its own predestined existence.

A lifeform which harnesses consciousness enjoys the cognition of an introspective personal identity, and the unique ability to *choose it's own destiny* (an advantage human beings enjoy apart from all non-conscious Earth-evolved lifeforms).

The Big Fucking Secret

Conscious human beings on Earth exist as an anomaly outside nature's automatic operating system, sprung forth to enable the spirit of the human race to advance in a limitless capacity at a non-predetermined pace.

From an old world 4th dimensional orientation with reality one would assert that human beings are a subject to nature, based on the human lifeform's current requirements of sun, water, and nutrition for survival, as well as natural resources from the Earth to facilitate civilization's advanced habitation.

But from a new world 5th dimensional orientation in which conscious control of existence is harnessed en masse, the human lifeform unravels itself from the conventions of nature, no longer shackled in pre-conscious evolutionary constraints.

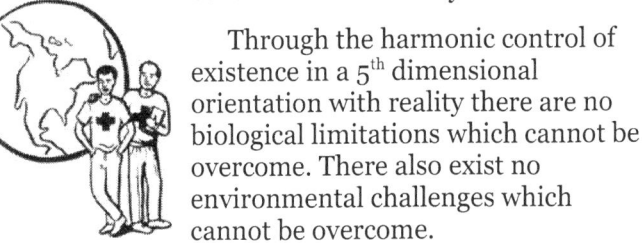

Through the harmonic control of existence in a 5th dimensional orientation with reality there are no biological limitations which cannot be overcome. There also exist no environmental challenges which cannot be overcome.

It's conceived through a 4th dimensional orientation with reality that Earth's eco-system is enduring eminent peril under the strain of an increasing population over-utilizing the available planetary resources. It's even irrationally asserted that human beings must stop procreating in order to avoid mass extinction.

There is no limit to the number of conscious beings a planetary system such as Earth may healthily support. And there is no limit to the abundance of resources which may be extracted to support their ability to thrive.

Eli Rook

We're observing the beginning of humanity's ability to achieve little or no-cost hydroponic production of essential nutrients through the advent of harnessing free energy, and utilizing nanotechnology to eliminate the biological legacy requirements to absorb nutrients. We're also seeing the onset of nanotechnology eliminating the need to consume Earth's physical resources for the production of durable goods.

With such conditions prevailing, the global adoption of a physically immortal mode of living among all conscious beings, Earth's eco-system can healthily support 10, 20, 50, 100 billion conscious beings, and beyond.

Esoteric Mysticism?

Your biological form is a product of nature, and you only harness consciousness in the mind after achieving the prerequisite linguistic skills.

Plus, early on in life, you "downgraded" to a 4th dimensional orientation with reality, which is subject to nature by default.

Therefore, that part of you which is still nature-driven – the elements of thought and biology you source exclusively from a 4th dimensional orientation with reality – are subject to the forces of nature, and are reflected in certain nature-sourced esoteric concepts.

The Big Fucking Secret

Because various "esoteric sciences", such as Astrology, I-Ching, Numerology, Feng Shui, Magik, and other Occult teachings, originate through conceptualizations of nature's phenomena, they apply to nature-sourced living organisms, including human beings.

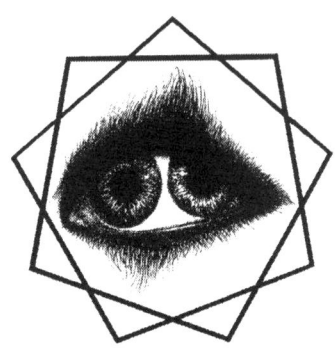

But, with your ascension into a 5th dimensional orientation with reality, you defy the conventions of predictable nature-bound esoterica.

From a 5th dimensional orientation with reality, the forces of nature in no way compare to the force you wield as a conscious being. Even the seemingly inescapable electromagnetic pull of celestial bodies persists without any effect on your thoughts and actions.

Astrology, I-Ching, Numerology, Feng Shui, Magik, and other Occult teachings are not in themselves mystical. Only a conscious being can be mystical. The degree of mysticism inherent in any conceptual body of knowledge is always subject to the beholder. Yet the validity of these "esoteric sciences" is only applicable to conscious beings suffering from the disease of the mind.

Eli Rook

When an individual consciously submits to the forces of nature expressed throughout esoteric teachings, that individual is living in contradiction to their nature as a conscious being – that individual is defaulting to *mysticism*.

But when esoterica is studied in an attempt to gain knowledge about how to increasingly gain control over nature – by ascending to a 5th dimensional orientation with reality – the value of esoterica is harnessed *as a technology*.

New Age Foibles

Although the intention behind most "New Age" spiritual teachings is meaningful and vibrant, gross errors contribute to their limited impact on civilization.

For instance, a misappropriation of language is used in most new age teachings which assert the human race lives in the 3rd dimension. This is imprecise, because if we lived in the third dimension we would be motionless, static objects.

Also, the assertion that the planet is in the third dimension and moving into the fourth is equally imprecise, for a planet, and nature itself for that matter, does not exist in any one dimension, and has no specific dimensional orientation.

Only conscious beings have the ability to consciously orient themselves within a specific dimension. And even in that capacity, it's only an *orientation* of the mind... The actual orientation of the conscious entity is always multidimensional.

The Big Fucking Secret

Using the term "conscious orientation with reality", and specifying 4th or 5th dimensional orientation is a precise, meaningful mode of communication that not only enhances the value of New Age texts, but serves to better bridge the wealth of New Age knowledge with establishment-biased scientific knowledge.

Science has been catching up with spirituality, and spirituality has been catching up with science…

The authors of The Big Fucking Secret believe that the precision in language and the solidification of certain basic concepts is necessary in bridging the gap between the two.

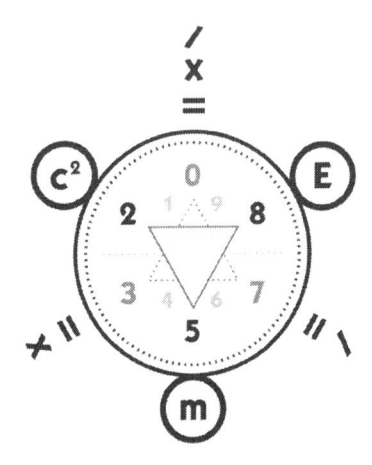

In addition, brands and movements crafted to be more accessible within the realm of popular culture, and marketed for mass consumption, further bridges that gap.

Creative content that induces quantum crossings amongst the masses must incorporate a formula of precision and accessibility that optimally obliterates the contradictions inherent in irrational religious doctrines, dishonest philosophical constructs, and pseudo-scientific "facts".

Eli Rook
Creation?

From the highest dimensional perspective (the recursive infinity of infinities of eternal multiverses which bare no beginning and no end) if every situation and circumstance experienced in existence by conscious beings has not only occurred, but occurred an endless number of times – with an endless degree of variables – how then would one consider any portion of existence to have been "created"?

All existence exists in multidimensional perpetuity.

Everything that *has* existed, or *will* exist, already exists in the multidimensional matrix... So for something to be created, it would have had to NOT EXIST prior to its creation.

Thus the concept of creation endures infinite regression loops, omnidimensional paradox, and progress-impeding "absolutes", which is why the authors chose to omit the words "create" and "creation" from this version of TBFS completely – instead using more precise language to navigate around the "creation paradox".

Currently, the authors conclude that creation is a metaphor applicable only to a fourth dimensional orientation with reality.

The conscious being sustaining a fifth dimensional orientation with reality creates NOTHING, and controls everything to render that which already exists in the multidimensional matrix.

The Big Fucking Secret

If all which is destined and accessible throughout the existence field already exists, the Pulsation of energy <u>conducted</u> by the conscious being merely <u>commands</u> forth all that is destined, <u>rendering</u> a unique life experience.

What's rendered is not precisely "created" as its existence was already omnidimensionally bonafide prior to the individual's experience.

Thus outside the narrow 4th dimensional conscious orientation of the individual plagued with the disease of the mind, the multidimensional reconciliation of "creation" metaphors remain broken.

Even the concept of belief becomes an archaic relic upon ascending into a 5th dimensional orientation with reality, as there is nothing but integrated honesty, and a life experience guided by degrees of favorable preference and desire.

All that which is destined and desired must come into the individual's life experience, and therefore it shall be. From such an ascended height of cognitive certainty, no aberration of degraded belief exists to which any desire may be inhibited.

Your Control of Existence

As each Planck unit is encountered, your life experience triangulates into a quantum position subsequent to the position you currently entertain.

Eli Rook

It's proposed that through your conscious immersion throughout the existence field you explode universe-containing gravity units within each Planck unit, customized to your Pulsation, which integrate holographically amongst all the previous universes you've existed within throughout the Planck "timeline" of your life experience.

Furthermore, each subsequent universe you exist within holographically intersects with the universes concurrently exploded by all the other conscious beings throughout the existence field, as they too encounter each subsequent Planck unit.

Your Pulsation is the determining factor through which other conscious beings conduct individual life experience intersecting your own. (Their residual self-images operate under the conditions endured within each multidimensional universe they explode, and those conditions are perfectly matched with the conditions within quantum position at any given moment).

Consciousness facilitates the multidimensional assembly of these fractalized universes throughout the multiverse, to be experienced individually by conscious beings as reality.

From an omnidimensional perspective, all potential universes which may exist are already coded throughout the endless matrix of existence (perhaps gravity-coded).

If so, you could potentially gain access to any of these universes based on the efficacy in which you harness consciousness to shift your quantum triangulation. Perhaps we have a little ways to go before possessing the tools to test such a theory =)

The Big Fucking Secret
Postulate Management

Throughout your life you've established an array of 5th dimensional postulates. Some have manifested, some have expired, some have been canceled, and some are still in the process of manifesting.

Take a moment to inventory the postulates you've consciously selected, like you were sitting in a satellite control center, reviewing the vital statistics of a communications network.

You can see which programs need more energy, which ones take priority over others, which ones have been fulfilled, and which ones need to be canceled as they no longer serve your favorable preferences.

If you're using The Self-Fulfillment Formula properly you should be focused on ONE SINGLE POSTULATE most of the time. It should come to mind immediately.

You should also be able to immediately pull up an inventory of exciting dreams – postulates you've established but do not consistently focus on because they have a lower priority than the ONE SINGLE POSTULATE you're always focusing on.

Upon searching, you will find memory of certain postulates you formed in the past, which have no way of physically transpiring under the current conditions of your life. When encountering these, be sure to consciously cancel them in order to free processing power in the brain.

Eli Rook

Destined Postulates

There are destined 5th dimensional postulates you are irrevocably bound to due to your nature as a conscious being, such as happiness, health, prosperity, romance, and safely.

Consider these fundamental destined 5th dimensional postulates you entertain to be the default features of the consciousness operating system. Right out of box the you're *guaranteed* to encounter the pursuit of these outcomes.

They're almost like the free software that comes with your computer's operating system. When conscious life is turned on, you automatically have access to these programs.

A destined 5th dimensional postulate is something that is not only possible due to its congruence with the laws of physics and its inevitability within the constraints of your Pulsation, but realistic based on the inalienable probability of it's outcome.

When you have established a fifth dimensional postulate, meaning you have built a replica of a future experience in your mind which holds 100% inevitability *(meaning there are NO inherent factors which may prevent it from transpiring),* you must understand that the imagined outcome *is* reality... It's reality in the 5th dimension.

The Big Fucking Secret
Rendering & Postulate Dynamics

When you consciously choose to change something in your life experience - putting the particles in motion to shift your quantum triangulation toward any desired outcome - you will not see instantaneous changes in your physical surroundings.

...There will be a *residue* of the the past *lingering* in your awareness. Don't confuse this as proof that *your will* is ineffective! Time must pass in order for your desires to render.

Your postulates may not render in your life experience for weeks, months, or years, but the postulate is certainly a component of 5th dimensional reality right NOW, and shall render as long as it remains destined.

Success is the pursuit of destined postulates, and if you're in constant pursuit, you must understand that your postulates ARE rendering. If you follow The Self-Fulfillment Formula correctly there shouldn't even be a trifle in this matter.

As time passes, if you do not exert the required effort (executing thoughts and actions) necessary for your postulate to render, the existence field will tirelessly recalculate alternate trajectories where you'll encounter ongoing situations and circumstances which lead to your postulate's manifestation.

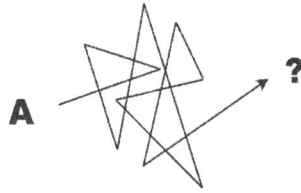

This is similar to how you might enter an destination address in your car's GPS navigation system, and if you miss a turn as you're driving, the navigation system will reroute you through the shortest alternative route available to compensate for your error, enabling you to get back on course.

But if you veer into unknown territory, the GPS will cease to provide directions until you return to a recognizable geographic coordinate.

Phantom Postulates

When conditions mount where a selected fifth dimensional postulate is no longer able to render in your life experience, it will expire.

The expiration of a postulate without your consent can cause unfavorable feelings in the body, as you brain is conducting an unreconciled energetic pattern which is incompatible with reality.

Take inventory of every objective postulate you've programmed into the existence field, and observe those which have transpired, those which have expired, and those which are still the progress of manifesting.

Also take inventory of the postulates you established which *seem to have expired*, but secretly persist outside the limited perception you held before reading The Big Fucking Secret.

The Big Fucking Secret

As your perception widens and these "phantom postulates" come back into view, identify the many situations and circumstances transpiring as a direct result of their bloom.

Note that when you're playing with 5th dimensional postulates that must transpire in a limited time frame, and you fail to exert the effort required to manifest the desired outcome, you risk the possibility of expiring the postulate. That's why, in the beginning, you want to experiment with postulates void of time constraints.

The All Is The Infinity Dimension

The Big Fucking Secret currently explains the multidimensional matrix of existence as being comprised of 10 distinct dimensions.

The fifth dimension is a realm of existence in which the endless possibilities related to an individual conscious being exist WITH REGARD to all that's transpired since the beginning of time, uniquely relative to that particular individual's life experience.

The sixth dimension is a realm of existence in which the endless possibilities related to an individual conscious being exist WITHOUT regard to all that's transpired since the beginning of time, uniquely relative to that particular individual's life experience.

The seventh dimension is a realm of existence in which the endless possibilities related to an individual conscious being exist without regard to the past, present, or future, and have an endless variety of DIFFERNT ENDINGS.

The eighth dimension is a realm of existence in which endless possibilities related to an individual conscious being exist without regard to the past, present or future, have an endless variety of different endings, AND an endless variety of different beginnings.

The ninth dimension is a ENDLESS realm of existence in which the eighth dimensional existence of an individual conscious being exists in an endless array of alternate forms, with no beginnings or endings.

And the tenth dimension is a realm of existence we can simply deem as infinity, because its endless iterations of 9th dimensional existence become recursive.

The Sixth Dimension

The sixth dimension is a realm of existence that boasts endless possibilities stretching backward in time, to effect the past, present, and future.

Your *orientation* within reality, the standpoint from which you control reality as an evolved conscious being having cured the disease of the mind, is – and always will be – a fifth dimensional orientation.

Under the model of an existence field constructed throughout ten dimensions, the tenth dimension is The All.

The Big Fucking Secret

The ninth dimension is a subset of The All, and the eighth dimension is a subset of the ninth. The seventh dimension is a subset of the eighth, and the sixth dimension is a subset of the seventh. The fifth dimension is a subset of the sixth, and the fourth dimension is a subset of the 5th.

It just so happens that while all these dimensions of existence are existing, the conscious being has the basic role of interacting with the existence field from a 5th dimensional (at best) orientation, or a 4th dimensional (at least) orientation.

Consciousness is multidimensional... it permeates ALL dimensions of existence... And you are a multidimensional conscious being.

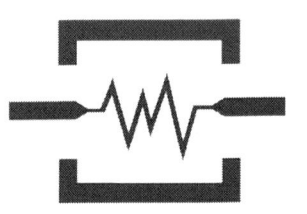

Through your Pulsation, you command sixth, seventh, eighth, ninth, and tenth dimensional potentiality. The entire existence field is being transfigured in regard to your unique life experience, as your Pulsation continues to render your life experience.

But as the eternal observer, you may only look to the fifth dimension to establish postulates which may be actively rendered in your experience. (If you had the ability to select and render 6th dimensional postulates you would potentially nullify all of your existing knowledge, relationships, or even your entire existence.)

$$\Delta\chi\Delta\rho \geq \frac{\hbar}{2}$$

Plus, sixth dimensional postulates carry the caveat that, as they render, your memory and cognition of the past must adhere to the newly established conditions regarding the rendering of the postulate[15].

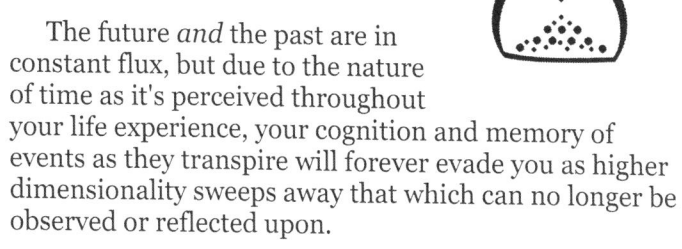

The future *and* the past are in constant flux, but due to the nature of time as it's perceived throughout your life experience, your cognition and memory of events as they transpire will forever evade you as higher dimensionality sweeps away that which can no longer be observed or reflected upon.

So yes, you command all the dimensions of existence to bend to your will, but only postulates which lie in the 5th dimension may be experienced in a manner which enables your conscious reflection upon the control of existence you wield[16].

The Utility of Fourth Dimensional Orientation

Gaining a complete 5th dimensional orientation does not mean that using the conscious mind to harness lower dimensional perspectives degrades the consciousness experience.

Be mindful that when you are oriented in 4, you are not oriented in 5. But when you are oriented in 5, you are *also* oriented in 4, 3, 2, and 1.

---

[15] A 2011 film titled "Source Code" presents a fictitious allegory describing this phenomenon.

[16] Also be mindful of the fact that a 5th dimensional postulate, at its core,

The Big Fucking Secret

Consider that within the 4th dimensional frequency range an individual can more effectively engage in meditative mind-clearing processes, sensory absorption, and certain modes of concentration.

With regard to such an example, accessing a 4th dimensional orientation with reality is not limiting the individual's capacity to fully engage in a disease-free consciousness experience, it's merely a mode utility in achieving a desired end result.

Spirit & Action

The individual life experience you entertain is a spiritually rich experience, but through the disease of the mind – being convinced that you are not God – a spiritual crisis ensues, in which the situations and circumstances you experience may be deemed unfavorable to your self, and even nature itself.

Thus your pursuit of a fifth dimensional conscious orientation with reality to cure the disease of the mind will restore the spirit of your life, and the spirit of all life throughout the cosmos, throughout the entire realm of existence you control.

The mind and body are inextricably linked, and the physical and the "spiritual" are also inextricably linked.

The experiences rendering in The All as a result of your pulsation is an expression of your spirit. And the more you conduct a life experience harmonically resonant with The All, the more your spirit is glorified.

When you are conscious of the fact that you are God, being active, working on creative projects, feeling good, and causing yourself to become more physiologically vibrant, you are reaching increasing symmetry with who you were meant to be (which is spiritual fulfillment).

The experience of being who you are meant to be is a physically-rooted experience, rich with the textures of third dimensional forms in constant flux. Physical reality is eternally embedded throughout all conscious experience. And spirit flows throughout in a symbiotic manner, without exception.

Immortality

It is documented that several millenia ago – before the leap into consciousness – pre-conscious human bodies, solely guided by nature's automatic guidance system, endured a lifespan of several hundred years.

The disease of the mind encountered upon the advent of consciousness, and its effect on human DNA, is the likely what caused the dramatic reduction of human lifespan.

While the complete transition into a 5th dimensional orientation with reality, a biological lifespan of several hundred years may again be restored, but technology-induced immortality is poised to solve the legacy issues in human biology throughout the next few decades.

The Big Fucking Secret
Success

Napoleon Hill, one of the most well regarded teachers on the subject of success, defined success as the "progressive realization of a worthwhile dream, or goal". In other words, success is a journey, not a destination.

Thus, success is a *state of being*.

Regardless of any current situations or circumstances being faced on planet Earth, all conscious beings are mentally and physically postured to enjoy increased happiness while engaging in success.

WINNING! (Duh!)

Success is NOT an *achievement*...

Success is NOT an *accomplishment*...

Success is the PROGRESSIVE REALIZATION of a worthwhile dream. Thus, success is conceived and sustained in the mind, while accomplishments and achievements are the RESULT of continued success.

You're either in the pursuit of a dream, or you're not. You're either in the act of consciously conducting your life toward the manifestation of your desires, or you're not. Being successful is intrinsic to the nature of conscious beings, as it's synonymous with the fulfillment of a conscious being's purpose for living – to be happy.

Those who are successful achieve greater symmetry with who they are meant to be ascend into greater spiritual fulfillment and individual power.

Eli Rook
Money

Money is a *technology* which - when honestly controlled - facilitates greater efficiency in the mutual exchange of value between two or more conscious beings. The exchange of value between conscious beings is how increasingly efficient life advantages are established in a rational civilization.

Technology, in all of its various manifestations, is a double-edged sword, used for good by rational conscious beings, and potentially used for evil by conscious beings acting irrationally in a 4th dimensional orientation with reality.

Because conscious beings are capable of empowering themselves to fulfill their desires with increasing speed using the technological benefits of money, one could propose that money is certainly used as an agreed upon medium of exchange in highly advanced civilizations; likely standardized through the measurement of energy units or gravity units (not fiat currencies such as those previously used on planet Earth).

Money possesses an awesome shape-shifting, transformative power no other physical form of matter possesses, as it can be converted in to almost any form of physical matter assembled outside of nature, and one could go as far as deeming money as the most virtuous form of physical matter conscious beings can possibly manifest because money is the preeminent form of physical matter most closely resembling energy itself.

The Big Fucking Secret

It's astounding to imagine the explosion of wealth that will transpire among all conscious beings on planet Earth when the agreed upon medium in which money is standardized changes from valueless fiat currencies to an objectively valued currency.

The sudden widespread use of honest money, such as decentralized independently issued digital currencies, would enable the human race to expediently vanish many of the unfavorable conditions that accrue from a lack of economic vibrancy.

Mythical External Influence of Others

No other conscious individual can "make" you, or anyone else do anything. You are in 100% control of reality, and so is every other conscious being.

You can be *coerced* for *forced* to do something against your most rational self-interest, but you only act in accordance the coercive and forceful to serve your own self-interest in surviving at the level you deem acceptable. You always have the option of rejecting anyone's attempt to coerce you or force you to do something – no matter what the consequences may be.

Mythical External Influence of Money

No physical object can "make you" do something. The idea that money "makes" people do things is postulated by individuals who are convinced that they are not God - convinced they have no control over their lives, or reality.

Some of the most vocal adversaries of the monetary form assert out of context rationalizations, such as genetics limitations in the human biology which restrict rational thought and activity upon exposure to the external influence of money.

But it is always the responsibility of a conscious being to think and act rationally, regardless of the physical reality they operate within, or the biological conditions they endure. Plus, the genetic argument against money is trumped by the fact that conscious beings ultimately control their DNA, and every conscious being has the power to subvert unfavorable inherited genetic influences with conscious thought alone.

In the new world order, vanquishing mythical conceptualizations in which external influences control conscious beings will guarantee eternal life, prosperity, and happiness.

Mind Control

If another individual suggests for you have a certain thought, which evokes an emotion, and results in an unfavorable feeling, the individual is in effect "making" you feel bad... because you cannot control the physiological reaction you experience when an emotion is evoked.

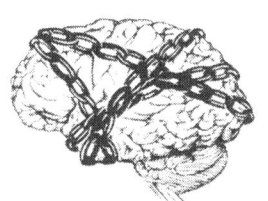

At the same time, it was you who manifested the situation where an another individual made the suggestion. Therefore, the feeling, the emotion, and the thought were are YOUR FAULT.

The Big Fucking Secret

It's popular to blame sources of information, like television media, as being "mind control". Yet the only mind control effecting an individual is self-induced.

Of course, any individual purposely attempting to make you feel bad should certainly be held accountable if you care to exert the effort, but your responsibility to be in control of your own life – no matter what - will never be extinguished, regardless of circumstance.

There can never be a victimizer without the sanction of the victim...

Consciousness / Self-Awareness

The definition of consciousness understood throughout popular culture now comes into greater clarity with the release of "The Big Fucking Secret".

Consciousness is not a physical part of the brain or the mind. Consciousness is woven throughout the existence field and it's harnessed through an organization of the mind facilitating the body's unique interface with The All.

By "plugging in" to access the controlling component of existence (consciousness) through the body/mind interface with existence you gain control of existence. You become God.

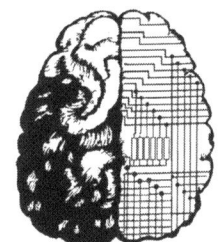

Self-awareness is not consciousness. Animals such as dolphins, primates, and dogs have been observed to display self awareness. Even non-biological entities such as robotic artificial intelligence have conclusively demonstrated self-awareness.

While conscious beings acquire an acute self-awareness, self-awareness alone is not indicative of consciousness. No other life form on planet Earth possesses the biological complexity to harness consciousness, to demonstrate introspective self-awareness and control existence on a quantum level outside of nature.

Mind Designations

Classic works such as Psycho-Cybernetics refer to the subconscious mind as the underlying operating system which is programed by the conscious mind.

Works in the area of Dianetics reference an analytical mind being the seat of one's I-ness, and the reactive mind as being inherent to the cellular makeup of an organism.

Julian Jaynes made reference to a bi-cameral mind as the mind which is void of consciousness, present in the brains of existing in all organisms, including modern human beings.

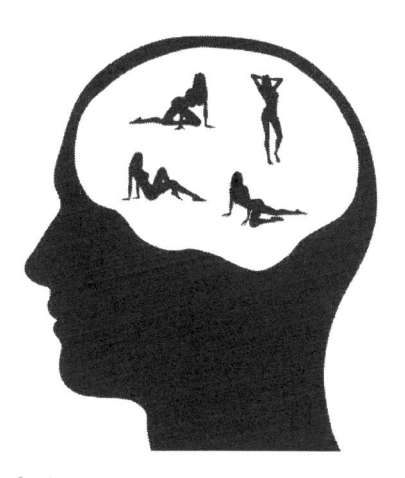

The Big Fucking Secret

The text of this book makes no reference to a subconscious mind, reactive mind, analytical mind, bicameral mind, or any other mind than the conscious and pre-conscious mind, not because of the imprecision of the before mentioned terms, but because the authors wish to produce a work that might add value to works which refer to various mind designations and their operational nuances.

The potential value of seeming contradictions which may arise through a reader's discernment between the information presented in The Big Fucking Secret and other works is intentional, and believed it to be a productive element adding value to one's quest to harness an understanding of consciousness.

False Ideas About Consciousness

Consciousness is regularly described as doing things and having characteristics it does not. Some examples of language incorrectly used regarding consciousness include:

"Consciousness is evolving. Consciousness if shifting. Consciousness is changing."

These descriptions are inaccurate and exemplify the thought process of someone who is convinced they are not God, believing they are subject to the "external force" of consciousness, higher powers controlling consciousness, or the *higher power of consciousness*.

Consciousness does not evolve, shift, or change. Consciousness is axiomatic, omnipresent, eternal; woven throughout the fabric of existence.

Human beings HARNESS consciousness through an organization of the mind, and therefore have the power to change, shift, and evolve their ABILITY to harness consciousness... but consciousness itself does not shift, change, or evolve.

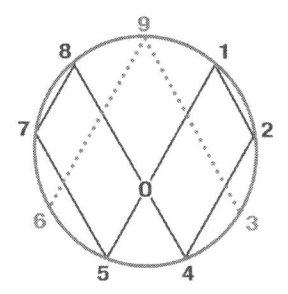

Claiming that consciousness evolves, shifts, or changes is like saying an automobile drives, brakes, and cleans itself.

No "Higher" Powers

No power in existence is stronger, greater, higher, or mightier than consciousness.

Consciousness is the controlling component of existence, woven throughout The All, harnessed by you, to be utilized in fulfilling your purpose as a conscious being.

The force of your individual consciousness, when fully harnessed, trumps ALL other forces in existence, including electromagnetic frequencies from technological devices, gravitational forces from the moon, planets, and other celestial bodies, and certainly other human beings not fully conscious of the fact that they are God.

The Big Fucking Secret

Even with regard to an idea where a "creator" was responsible for the existence of the human race, just as your parents were responsible for you, does not put that "creator" in any position of greater *capacity* for harnessing power than your own.

Because you became conscious, and for no other reason, you are on a level playing field with every other "creative" being in existence. You have the same capacity to harness power as any other intelligence in existence, and your ascension to a 5th dimensional orientation with reality is the final leap you'll endure toward harnessing that power.

God/Exo-God Modifier

Old world religious texts hold immense value as they spring into new meaning with your cognitions about the controlling utility woven throughout the existence field, harnessed by consciousness beings.

One may remain stuck in the contradictions that arise from a lack of honestly integrated knowledge about existence when observing religious texts in the context of old-world 4th dimensional perspectives.

But upon understanding The Big Fucking Secret, dogmatic religious texts spring into an entirely different light, which may have previously hindered in both theistic and non-theistic 4th dimensional orientations with reality.

Eli Rook
Atlantean & Ancient Astronaut Revisionist History

Popular revisionist accounts of history involving legends of Atlanteans and Alien Astronauts are 100% compatible with The Big Fucking Secret, if they are in fact accurate.

The evolution into consciousness is certainly historically evident, and if factors surrounding that phenomenon were in any way influenced by lifeforms who achieved consciousness long before the majority of civilization on planet Earth, the degree of accuracy expressed throughout this book will still remain.

Conscious Civilizations

While there are civilizations of conscious beings millions of years more advanced than the newly conscious civilization currently present here on planet Earth, the "higher power" of a highly advanced civilization is no different than the higher power of a billionaire philanthropist standing beside a fast food restaurant employee.

Both individuals have the same capacity to harness conscious control of nature, yet one has successfully exerted the effort to produce more measurable results that positively impact more lives than the other.

The Big Fucking Secret

Ultimately, the only three things distinguishing the level of advancement between an two or more individual conscious beings, and even the level of advancement between two or more conscious civilizations, is a boldness of intention, a loyalty to honesty, and time.

Conscious civilization on Earth today has ready access to the physical resources necessary to harness control of nature to access endless free energy, enjoy rapidly advancing technologies, quickly clean up the planet, cure all diseases, and enable every conscious being on the planet to enjoy prosperity, safety, and immortality.

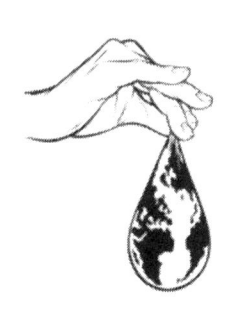

Progress requires no higher power than the power contributed by each individual conscious being engaging in success toward their purpose in life.

Level Playing Field

With your personal discovery of the fact that you are God, there are no substantial limitations in your life to have, be, or do anything and everything you want.

You have no incentive to remain in a semiconscious holding pattern any longer.

Through and honest and rational conceptualization of reality, each new thought springing forth from your mind, and each new quantum position you endure, enriches the entire existence field.

Eli Rook

This experience called life is your magnum opus, a sweet and sour symphony played gracefully as you dance your way through the luminous beauty of the multiverse.

It is our sincere wish you begin actively transforming your life on planet Earth for the betterment of all – with a tenacious belief in the power of God.

We hope to hear about all your amazing experiences at BigFuckingSecret.com

The Big Fucking Secret

Eli Rook

WORD OF ADVICE

With most conscious beings on planet Earth convinced that they are not God, expect the vast majority of conscious beings you encounter to have not yet reached the orientation with reality you now hold.

(Feel good knowing this is changing.)

Even though the majority of conscious beings on Earth have the consciousness disease of believing outside influences and external forces control their lives, individuals are recovering from the disease daily, and the observed recovery is succeeding in exponential fashion.

Being aware of the fact that other conscious beings are still not conscious of the fact that they are God puts you in a role of leadership. *As a leader you should never try to convince anyone that they are God.*

Only someone who considers the possibility that they are God, and seeks further understanding will endure the experience in their life where they obtain the knowledge you now possess.

Any individual crusade you venture on will surely fail if you attempt to convince anyone to change how they orient themselves with reality.

So as a suggestion, if you wish to channel your enthusiasm for this book into productive results, you should consider being a promoter of the book, not a preacher.

This book has been tediously designed to take the reader through a permanent consciousness altering experience, where quantum crossings are induced from a 4th dimensional orientation with reality to a 5th dimensional orientation with reality.

If you truly want others to have the benefit of being able to think like you think, you could certainly share this book with them, or give them a copy as a gift...

But please allow others the blessing of discovering the fact they are God on their own, without being proselytized. *Consider being zealous without becoming a zealot.*

Your ability to follow this suggestion will surely bring illuminating abundance into your life, and the lives of all those you care for.

If you wish to purchase bulk copies of The Big Fucking Secret at discounted wholesale prices, in quantities of 10, 50, 100, or more, you'll find ordering instructions at BigFuckingSecret.com

Eli Rook

The Big Fucking Secret

Eli Rook

WARNING

Eli Rook is not your fucking GURU!

The authors of "The Big Fucking Secret" do not purport to be masters of this information, and instead humbly assume a position right beside you, as being students open to *all* knowledge and wisdom.

The authors express their integrations of knowledge throughout the pages of this book, with the intention to benefit all those who read, but assume no guru-ship, or infallibility in any area of life.

Every word of encouragement and ever blasphemous condemnation is aimed at both the readers AND the authors, as all conscious beings co-exist in ascension.

The Big Fucking Secret is a work of *literary art*, in perpetual development. It will change as time passes, errors will be corrected, and content will be reformed to best serve the needs of its collective readership.

All ideas presented have been swiped, remixed, transmuted, and shamelessly racked from a variety of sources the authors have encountered throughout their lives.

Eli Rook could have grifted a ton money by purporting this book was channeled from spirit beings, acquired from aliens, or obtained by infiltrating the clandestine libraries of ancient secret societies, but it's simply a collection of vastly integrated knowledge, put together by individuals just like you.

The Big Fucking Secret

The contents are intended for mass consuption by an audience of misfit geniuses, who hold a vision of an honest, sovereign world, and will eagerly contribute the sweat equity required to manifest it.

We hope the contents enrich your life, and assist you in rendering the Civilization of Luminiferous Ascension with accelerating speed.

If you want to offer some appreciative or constructive feedback, drop a line to:

feedback@bigfuckingsecret.com

We read all the incoming messages and respond to many.

Eli Rook

YOU

ARE

GOD

BigFuckingSecret.com

Made in the USA
Lexington, KY
13 October 2012